PORTRAIT
of a
FEMINIST

PORTRAIT
of a
FEMINIST

A Memoir in Essays

Marianna Marlowe

SHE WRITES PRESS

Published 2025
Printed in the United States of America
Print ISBN: 978-1-64742-752-8
E-ISBN: 978-1-64742-753-5
Library of Congress Control Number: 2024918847

For information, address:
She Writes Press
1569 Solano Ave #546
Berkeley, CA 94707

Interior design by Stacey Aaronson

She Writes Press is a division of SparkPoint Studio, LLC.

To All Feminists Everywhere: Past, Present, and Future

CONTENTS

PORTRAIT
of a
FEMINIST

Feminist or Not?

(*California, 2013*)

I scan the formal dining room. Twelve young faces look back at me, expectant. The group is all girls, all of them long-haired and most of them pony tailed, all but one white. This is a National Junior League meeting a friend of mine asked me to lead. Her daughter, blonde as well as long-haired and pony tailed, sits among the others at the polished mahogany table. I have two hours to teach them about media literacy.

What I'm desperate to teach these girls is how to read the "texts" surrounding them every day and everywhere: the advertisements, romance novels, billboards, songs, and music videos, the movies, television shows, fashion magazines, Super Bowl commercials, and makeup tutorials, the Barbies and dolls and mannequins that all contain coded and uncoded messages about them—how they, young women, should look and behave, what they should want, what they should put up with, why they should be ashamed. I want them to see the ever-present influences of our patriarchal culture, the ones working their spells, saturating every part of our social ecosystem like powerful dye tainting a bowl of water—or, even more fittingly I think, like toxic bacteria colonizing a host body.

I start by asking the question I used to ask my college classes at the beginning of each semester, "Who here is a feminist?"

Almost immediately, a hand shoots up. It belongs to the stocky, athletic girl at the table. After a moment's hesitation, during which they see this first girl's hand in the air, two more girls, still tentative, raise their hands.

My eyes scan the group of young women once again, hoping for another hand. No one else moves.

I sigh—but only on the inside, of course. I'd hoped that in the ten years that have passed since I taught undergraduate courses, the culture would have changed more than it has, much more than three raised hands, two of which are ambivalent.

Regardless, I do what I always do, I do the only thing I can think to do: I launch into the lesson.

Part One

SEEDS PLANTED

In the Beginning

(California, 1971)

$\mathcal{I}$ sit on the toilet seat in our Jack-and-Jill bathroom, writing as furiously as a five-year-old can write. I'm in a hurry — worried and sad. I clutch at the crayon, pressing hard on the unlined paper. It is a letter I'm writing. What heading do I give it? *Dear Aunt Clara? Dear Tía Clara? Dear Clara?* Probably the latter. Because I live in the US, speak English, and never learned to call my Peruvian aunt "tía" — despite my mother speaking only Spanish to me — it must be *Dear Clara.*

I'm halfway through the scrawled letter when my mother comes into the bathroom to find me.

My mother always knew, even if vaguely, where I was. She was attuned to me, just as I was attuned to her. Not quite at the same level, to be sure, for I was a vibrating antenna, always pointed in her direction, registering her whereabouts, her activities, her moods. And she, by that time, already had another child who needed her love and attention.

When she sees me on the toilet seat, writing instrument in hand, she gives a little exclamation of surprise and pulls the paper gently from my fingers. It only takes her a few seconds to get the gist of the contents, to understand that her young daughter has been writing to her sister who lives thousands of miles, a different hemisphere, and a three-hour time zone away to ask for money. I'm asking for money, she reads, because she, my mother, needs it. She needs it because my father won't give her any.

Did I write *Papá* or *Father* or *Daddy*? Of course Daddy. At five, and speaking mostly English, why would I think to write anything else? That's what I called him then. Although now, whenever I think of him in the past, I think of him as "my father," and have called him "Dad" for years. When I look back at him as the father of my childhood, he is a tall, quiet presence in my life, serious and authoritarian, a man with whom rules are to be followed, chores to be done, orders to be obeyed.

"Daddy" won't give "Mommy" the money she needs. I can hear them out in the kitchen, beyond the closed door of the bathroom. They are fighting. They always argue in Spanish, which is the language of their marriage. I'll learn later that once my American father became engaged to my mother, he traveled to Peru to take a crash course in her native tongue, and always spoke it with her thereafter.

Although I choose not to speak Spanish most of the time, I can, and am fluent in understanding it. So I know my mother wants cash from my father, who controls the money and makes all the final decisions about finances. In this instance, he doesn't feel she has a good case. She doesn't need the money, only wants it. And they are on a budget. "The house" cannot afford it. It is clear to my mother, as she tries to convince my father to give her some, that she won't get it.

I hear from the tone of her voice that she really needs it and Daddy won't give it to her because . . . I don't know why, but I think in my head that he is mean. He's so *mean*. He's mean to my mother and my mother is sad and she needs the money. But my aunt has money. I know because I'm familiar with her house in the suburbs of Lima. I've watched from the backseat as the guard runs to open the gate when he recognizes my aunt at the wheel. I've seen the cars and the servants and the fountain and the silver. I've looked on as she has sorted through her jewelry in the wide shallow drawers designed for easy access; I've watched her spray herself with the perfumes lined up on the bathroom shelf. She is rich. I'm sure she has extra money to give to my mother.

Could she send some right away? *¿Por favor?*

My mother laughs a little laugh of shock and gratification as her eyes finish scanning the creased paper. *"Ay, mi vida,"* she says. *"¿Qué estás pensando? Tenemos suficiente plata. No te preocupes."*

And she keeps the paper, my messy, half-written letter, and crumples it up, and throws it away.

*M*y husband hears me talk about this long-ago event when I sat in the single bathroom of my family's cottage, on the toilet seat, trying to craft a letter to an aunt I saw as a rescuing angel.

"That's impressive," he says. "You have such a good memory. How can you remember so far back?"

I think for a moment. "Because I was traumatized," I finally say.

I was traumatized by watching my mother's pain, by feeling responsible for alleviating it, for taking it away, for finding a solution. And the enemy, the source of the problem, always seemed to be my father. I saw it in the bickering and arguing and fighting, I felt it in their silences and dagger eyes and stony faces. I knew it for sure when my mother complained to me about him, her rigid and implacable Anglo husband, using me as a sounding board and best friend and confessor.

If Spanish was the language of my parents' marriage, then in those days, when I was a young child, during the time of my earliest memories, the kitchen was the room of my parents' relationship. The wooden table where we sat together for our meals as a family could have worked as a metaphor except that my parents' marriage needed more space to manifest itself, to show how it functioned—its push and pull, friction and conflict. And in that kitchen I was the sponge that wiped up the mess and absorbed the tension and got squeezed into the sink to slide down the drain, and I was also a container that received the matter, the material, of my parents' anger and held it, tight and safe, keeping it for my mother. My parents' dissatisfaction with each other dripped and fell and spread over the surfaces, the wooden table, the laminated counters, the vinyl floor. Someone had to clean it up, and the task fell to me—or I accepted it, maybe even embraced it, grasping it to me and hugging it tight.

I was the oldest child, and so close to my mother that some-times I didn't know where I ended and she began. When her voice broke, my heart constricted. When she was sad, I cried. When she was in trouble, I wrote a letter to her sister, her older sister who was rich and powerful and loved my mother without bossing her around or denying her anything. I was the sponge, I was the sink, I was the drain, I was the container—the pitcher or the bucket or the tub—the final resting place of my mother's frustration and powerlessness in the face of my father's stubborn need to control.

For years I babysat for a young family with an only daugh-ter, starting when she was a few months old and continuing into her tweens. Her mother, who for a while dabbled in Jungian psychology, commented often on my family's dynamics.

"You and your sister are way too close to your mother," she'd say. "You're too old to be so enmeshed. You need to have more boundaries."

I would look at her as she spoke, oh so confidently, about my family that, yes, she knew fairly well, but which she judged from an alien perspective, from the viewpoint of a diametrically opposed culture. *Ha*, I thought to myself, *you don't know what you're talking about. Even though you were one of eight children, you spent your adolescence alone in boarding school on the East Coast. No one cared about you the way my mother, who is warm and loving and Peruvian, cares about us.* And I was smug and satisfied in our lack of boundaries, in my closeness to my mother, in her vast, unconditional love for me and my sister and my brother.

I know now I am more like my father, in personality and even in looks, but my entire childhood was my mother's. I belonged to her—body, mind, and soul. I was making myself into her image. Watching and waiting and wanting, observing and emulating. As the birthdays passed, numbers six-seven-eight-nine, her tastes became mine, her values my own, her wishes always my commands.

My father was the Other. He was the opposite of my mother, her antithesis; all of their differences were polarized for me as a child. If, when I was young, I'd had to choose between my mother and my father in any scenario, from sleeping in the same bed or driving around with them on errands to divorce or a sinking ship, I would have chosen my mother. Every time. It took years into adulthood for me to see my father as an individual free from the mantle of my mother's desires and disappointments.

I would say, if it were possible, that I was born a feminist. I feel it in my bones, in my core, in my very Self. Because mine is a feminism that cannot bear injustice, it was my defining identity growing up, in school, out clubbing, as a graduate student, dating and courting and marrying, as a wife and mother, an intellectual and scholar. Watching my parents interact, sensing the tension between the easygoing extrovert who felt comfortable in domestic chaos and rejuvenated by parties and music and dancing versus the introverted loner who needed everything neat and tidy and quiet regardless of his wife's desires or children's personalities, served to feed that feminism like fresh soil around a plant and sharpen it like a blade on a stone. Growing up, I felt as if I were watching a game, or a boxing match, and my mother was clearly the underdog. She didn't hold the purse strings and therefore she didn't hold the power. My father's word was, without exception, the last; it was his way or the highway every time. I'd watch and root for my mother, demonizing my father as her opponent, especially when, as I grew into adolescence, I jumped into the ring to defend her—always to no avail.

The thing is, I was my mother's second-in-command, her assistant coach, her Girl Friday. Also her therapist, priest, and close confidant. If early experiences shape a self, guide a growing, developing identity, then my mother, my parents, and, most of all, their relationship to each other, shaped me. Their marriage took my feminism, that innate sense of justice untempered by rationalizations, excuses, lies, or obfuscations, and shaped it through the template of their relationship, ultimately as witness for and defender of my mother.

*O*ur skin sloughs off day by day and month by month until some time later we are totally different people: hair, skin, nails, all new—nothing left over from the past. Recently there has been scientific talk of our changing in more essential ways throughout our lives, not just surface characteristics but also outlook, values, sense of self—our very subject-ness. Like a snake we shed not only our skin but also our old selves, our former personas, including our ignorance, our biases, our humiliations, and our embarrassments. I resist this, however compelling it is to believe in continuous opportunities for renewal and redemption. I need to feel I have a core, an essence, indelible and unassailable. I hold on to this belief even if by doing so I condemn myself to the initial molding of my childhood, when my parents and their personalities, their interactions, and their marriage branded me in ways that will forever mark me — how I think, the nature of my feminism.

My mother, if asked, would have rejected outright the label of "Feminist." She would have thought feminists in the seventies weird white women — American, loud, and unfeminine. She still calls opinionated women "*sargentos*" and protesting feminists who behaved "*como hombres*" fit this definition, shouting in the streets with their signs and their slogans. My mother had an aunt who advocated bra wearing rather than bra burning. She advised wearing a bra twenty-four hours a day, seven days a week, even to bed, in order to keep the breasts high and perky in defiance of nursing and gravity. My mother followed this advice for many years, as did I, having also in my late teens received the lecture on the power of the brassiere.

Yet my mother did not remain passive in the face of my father's dominance. She fought for control, trying to seize agency in the areas that mattered to her most. She wanted a say in the finances, for example, in the ways my father's salary was budgeted for the household. With a keen eye for real estate, she wanted to invest in certain properties and loved the idea of the fixer-upper long before it became a trend. She wanted to buy herself and her daughters new, fashionable clothes more often. She wanted to spend money on airline tickets, to visit her sister. But my father allotted an allowance for himself and his wife, refusing her access to the bank account.

I, like many others, was fired in the clay oven of my nuclear family. It was because of them that I entered the world, finally, as an adult, the way I did. These true stories reflect that early molding, and also bear witness to the myriad other influences in the continuing evolution of the feminist I am today. I can never be sure how much of myself was modeled and framed, measured and cut by growing up in my particular family, observing my parents, loving my mother, and how much by the combination of other factors in life—a specific set of genes and a collection of experiences unique to me.

In trying to envision the ways my feminism developed, starting from my very earliest memories, there first comes to mind, sadly, the image of a gauntlet run: veering from, sometimes colliding with, unhappy moments and flagrant unfairness. But there are also the more pleasing, more satisfying images of the mosaic and the stones, the collage and the pictures, and, ultimately, the narrative and the words. Selecting the words, creating a narrative. This time with penned notes or typed documents rather than crayon on scratch paper, and at a desk or on a couch or in my bed rather than on the closed seat of a porcelain toilet. Writing for myself this time rather than on behalf of my mother.

Thinking about my past, pondering why I remember what I do, and examining those memories is a journey. The words, the paragraphs, the essays make up my path. Any answers, regardless of how incomplete or continuing or exploratory, to how my feminism developed, what is its complicated and shifting nature—the holy grail.

The Book and the Scarf

(*United States, 1965*)

A woman sits, seat belt securely fastened, in an airplane. She is crying. Tears flow, almost uninterrupted, for hours on the flight from Peru to the United States. From Lima to New York. From Jorge Chavez to JFK on her way to SFO. Her nose swells, her eyes puff, her head aches.

Why does she weep? She cries because she is leaving her family forever. This is different from when she left Peru the first time, for what she assumed would be only a few years. Now she is marrying an American she met in the United States and committing to a life far away from her home. She is sad because she is already homesick, knowing she will speak to her mother and sister on the telephone only a few times a year, the connection unreliable and the cost prohibitive. Knowing she will visit her city, with its warm sociability and carefree lifestyle, at most once a year, the cost of flights astronomical. Knowing she has chosen a man different from her own Italian father and a culture opposite of her own Peruvian one—reserved rather than open, straitlaced rather than easygoing, more individualistic than familial.

Some years prior, a young man stands on the deck of a large ship that travels slowly west toward Japan, where he will be stationed as a military engineer for the duration of the Korean

War. The ship passes San Francisco and continues under the Golden Gate Bridge—perhaps it is early morning and the pale mist wraps around the still-sleeping city, covering the bay, softening the angles of the handful of huddled skyscrapers; perhaps it's high noon on a summer day and he sees the brightness of the blue sky highlighting the shifting green of the sea, the clean white of the cityscape, the rusty red of the bridge; or perhaps the sun is setting and rendering him privy to the city's buildings, with Coit Tower the most distinguished, lit up by the sun as if from within, glowing bright and then softening to pinks and golds and oranges. Whichever the scenario, whatever the time of day, this man, my father, remembers looking out from the deck of the ship taking him toward the unknown, toward a yet undefined adventure, and thinking to himself, *One day I will return.*

The woman who wept, my mother, lived for several years before her marriage in the "Pink Palace," an elegant residential hotel in Pacific Heights. She has pointed it out to me from the car innumerable times, a still-standing monument, a tangible testament, all pink stucco and wrought iron and marble, to her single life in San Francisco, where she claims to have lived in the best neighborhood, worn the most stylish clothes, and frequented the classiest venues. It is there that she met her future husband, my father. Because his residence, located nearby, did not provide breakfast, he made it a habit to eat at my mother's hotel every morning. She claims he noticed her first, that he made the first move. I can believe that; although my father is an introvert, quiet and reserved, this was the early sixties after all, and both of them were more *Mad Men* than Summer of Love. My mother—pretty, foreign, glamorous—must have stood out to him as he drank his coffee and read the newspaper.

In his retirement, my father has been looking through his collection of old slides. This activity prompted a memory he tells me about: "The first time I saw your mother she was sitting in the basement under a giant hair dryer. She was reading *Don Quixote* in Spanish. That's when I thought, she's beautiful *and* smart!"

My mother married my father because he was good on paper—tall, dark, and handsome, an engineer—and unfailingly polite. Her mother, my grandmother, had sent her younger daughter to live in the United States when she decided it was time for her to find a husband. My mother told my grandmother she was happy to live with her in Lima for the rest of her life, but her arguments were to no avail. My grandmother remained convinced that a life as a single, childless woman was not one worth living, and refused to be responsible for my mother's unmarried status. So she sent her daughter away to find a man outside Peru. And she did.

My father courted my mother. On one of their formal dates, they went to a performance of *My Fair Lady*. I can see them, my mother in a simple silk sheath, pointed heels, and pearls, my father in a dark suit, leather wingtips, and a thin tie. At the end of the night, my mother expressed her delight with the play. The next day she received a gorgeously wrapped copy of the text inscribed, "To G, with love B."

My father grew up with a strict British mother from York-shire. He expected an efficient household, run with the minimum of fuss and the maximum of frugality. Dinner meant a salad, a starch, a vegetable, and a meat set on the table at seven in the evening, not before and not after. My mother was brought up with servants; my father had to show her how to boil an egg. In Peru, friends and family gathered spontaneously. Lima's high society in the fifties and sixties was fluid when it came to punctuality, and being an hour or two late was negligible, not worth registering. My mother, a product of this culture, never served dinner on time. If, on a rare occasion, dinner was ready close to seven, the meat was tough and charred or raw and bloody. My father—the lover of ritual and routine who woke up at the same exact time, who did the same boot camp exercises every morning, who breakfasted on two perfectly soft-boiled eggs and two pieces of thickly buttered toast with a tall glass of orange juice and a mug of coffee every single day, made my mother—the lover of spontaneity, the impulsive shopper, the eschewer of timetables, the yo-yo dieter, the easy, natural, take-each-day-as-it-comes personality—his wife.

On their honeymoon, the day after they arrive at the Bahamian island of St. John's, my mother stops at a stall selling colorful silk scarves. "Oh!" she says, pointing one out to her brand-new husband, "I'd love to have this one!"

His answer? "Buy it with your allowance."

It was as if, she always tells me, my father had thrown a glass of cold water in her face. The courtship was over.

At the Columbian Hotel

(Columbia, 1978)

*W*hat I remember about the resort hotel, besides its quiet modernity, its white walls and wide porch, its open dining hall with views of the watery green outside, is what I heard in the room I shared with my family, the five of us crowded onto two beds. It wasn't sharing a bed with my mother or father or siblings that is memorable for me, as that was normal for us. Before we moved from California to Ecuador for my father's job, our entire family slept in two beds and a crib pushed together, with the children, including my little brother (for whom the rejected crib was intended), bickering every night about who got to sleep next to our mother. In Quito, at ten years old, I finally graduated to my own room, but I didn't always appreciate it, feeling sometimes lonely in my twin bed—the space around me too large, the night too quiet.

What I remember from that one night in the Columbian hotel, during the rainy season somewhere in the lush countryside north of the Ecuadorian border, are the moans I could hear from the adjoining room: rough, primal, and rhythmic, they permeated the hotel's thin walls. Female and pained, they penetrated the darkness, itself so deep and palpable, around us. Then they stopped and I heard instead the creak of bedsprings.

A woman murmured in soft Spanish, "Come back . . . I'm sorry . . . I'm sorry. Let's try again." Then once more the silence punctured by the moans that emanated as reliably as the ticking of a long hand circling the face of a clock.

What I couldn't imagine then, but can now: the adjacent hotel room, the king bed in the middle, the man—methodical, silent, selfish, and the woman—crying out but trying not to.

Innocence Lost

(Quito, 1980)

*T*here must have been a noise, a rustle or a snapping of twigs underfoot. Something that made me look to my left as we—my best friend Sarah, our young redheaded teacher, and I—hiked up the path through the forest. Like an animal in the wilderness, it was instinctual, the quick turn of head, the sudden attention to the unexpected. My eyes focused on the source of the sound until I registered a male figure, fuzzy in the background and, in the foreground . . . a penis. It dominated my vision like a snake, pallid underbelly framed by a bush of black hair.

I don't remember reacting. Although from a bird's-eye view I was the prey and the man the predator, the natural instincts telling me to run, scream, or warn the others receded and were replaced by the social ones I'd already begun to internalize as a young girl. So I looked away from the man leering at us through the leafy branches and, without a word, focused instead on the path before me.

The mountain is actually a volcano, a solid pyramid looking over Quito, a dependable constant in the landscape of the small Andean city. So familiar a sight was it to me, as I lived my life across the valley below, that I often forgot it was there. But that day, for the first time, I was hiking it. My friend and I, both in eighth grade, had earned a fun day out with a young teacher new to the missionary school we attended.

Thinking back, I wonder at the innocence with which we set forth—three young females, one in her twenties, white and freckled and obviously American, and two in their tweens, awkwardly transitioning through puberty. The teacher, the only adult, was young and naïve, a guaranteed virgin of the fervid Evangelical type, modest in her hiking pants, covered arms, and short haircut. There was nothing provocative about her, even her hair was more faded strawberry than fiery red. But it was her race and her gender together in one persona—single white female—that made our presence in the mountain forest of the Andes so strange. That day, even when I saw the man's nakedness among the woody undergrowth, I had no conscious awareness of our vulnerability; the fear lay still, buried deep inside my psyche, a mute sense of foreboding rather than the sharp recognition of danger. Because I chose then to remain quiet, I don't know if either of my companions saw what I did—it happened so suddenly, the moment over almost before it began.

Another day, walking from school through residential streets to my friend Julia's house, I helped form another three-some, this time with Julia and her older sister, Fatima. Unlike Sarah, who was pale and blonde, Julia and Fatima were dark, darker than me. They favored their mother. With their matte-brown skin and heavy black hair, they looked more like the maid who cleaned their house than the father who paid for it, a wealthy American businessman working abroad. I was more familiar with this maid, who cracked eggs into bubbling oil for us to eat with salty white rice as a snack, than with their mother, similarly brown and Ecuadorian, who seemed always away, absent, in another room.

There were plenty of rooms to hide in at Julia and Fatima's

house; oversized for a family of four, it had a garden wall topped with the requisite shards of glass, a spiked gate guarding the long driveway, carved doors at the entrance, and an indoor/outdoor pool, loosely S-shaped, winding its way outside from under sliding glass panes. I had never met the father, had only ever seen him once—at his house, during a school party that spilled over into the evening. He had stepped onto a balcony overlooking the pool that was lit from the inside, clear water shining in the inky night. A shadowy figure, cocktail in hand, he hesitated at the railing, swaying . . . was he about to say something? But he did not. He continued to gaze down at us instead, at our pubescent bodies undulating in the watery light and shivering in the evening air, thin wet suits clinging to barely there curves. After a while, mere seconds or whole minutes I will never know now, he retreated, with a slight stumble, to the darkness of his bedroom. Thinking back, it could be that the goose-bumped flesh that I, so young at the time, didn't know could tantalize certain men, tantalized him. Or it could be that he was lonely and drank nightly to numb feelings of isolation and distance from his wife, his family, even his adopted culture. But my recollections of that evening pose him as a menacing figure—a man threatening us from above, master of his universe, the balcony his throne—and an untrustworthy adult, drunk and unstable, a father gone wrong.

That day after school, still blocks from the house, the older sister Fatima walked a few yards ahead of my friend Julia and me. Then, quite suddenly, she pivoted mid-stride to face the opposite sidewalk. Catching up to her, we saw what she saw: a man standing in an empty lot between residences, legs planted wide, ignoring the NO ORINE AQUÍ scrawled on a peeling wall as yellow liquid slid down the chipped concrete to disappear among weeds and emptied soda cans. A second later he must have sensed our presence, because he turned and saw that we were watching him. With his pants still crumpled around his knees, he thrust his groin forward, grinning. I stood silently while I looked, Julia quiet beside me, both of us stunned into a kind of paralysis.

Fatima, however, wasn't stunned or silenced. Instead, with her younger sister and me helpless behind her, she pointed a cocky finger at the man and shouted at him in Spanish. She made fun of his penis, mocking him, humiliating him. Her words and her stance, her *attitude*—so different from my own—worked like a counterspell to block the man's attempt to intimidate us. He turned away, yanking up his trousers, fumbling at his belt.

Fatima at that moment seemed to me a superhero, a woman warrior. She had conquered the foe, beaten the enemy. His sudden retreat gave all three of us an unfamiliar sense of power, and we raced the rest of the way home, laughing with exhilaration.

*D*ecades after and thousands of miles away, back in the United States, I flick through a glossy *National Geographic*. I almost don't recognize it. At the last minute, I flip back to a page I've just passed over in my casual perusal of the magazine. Something about the image of a volcano erupting pulls at my consciousness. The caption below the photograph verifies that it's the mountain I hiked so many years ago, as a child. Here, however, the city is assaulted by a storm of thick smoke and black ash as hot clouds obliterate the sun. The mountain has transformed into a raging monster. In the foreground, a woman waits patiently for a bus in the valley beneath. This woman is indigenous: short and stocky, brown-skinned, face prematurely lined, wearing coarse stockings and shoes cracked from her splayed feet. One hand holds a plastic shopping bag straining against its heavy load, the other an open umbrella. Years from now, I will remember the umbrella as red. Perhaps it wasn't red, it might have been blue or black. But my memory will insist on red, a bright red that becomes a steady beacon of color pushing back against the swirling ash, protecting the woman who holds it.

Why this connection in my memory between my coming-of-age in Ecuador and this mountain? Why the association of eroded innocence with the volcano, active after decades of quiet? If I think of this time in my life, the pubescence that is a limbo between childhood and adolescence, as a dark fairy tale replete with serpents, evil kings, hunters in the woods, and monstrous mountains, then I am Freud, analyst and decoder, attempting to make sense of the past and the innocence that was lost. A mountain—once dependable, firm, and stable, a benign presence, a benevolent god—turns villainous, threatening to overwhelm the woman, already burdened.

But is she, like I once was, wracked with insecurity, with fear? No. She stands instead, steadily holding the umbrella that protects her. An umbrella that is always red—the red of blood, and thus violence and gore and wounds, but also of menstruation, life, creation. This is the connection that speaks to me today: innocence lost, yes, and many times over, but also resistance and pushback, the promise of power gained.

The Kiss

(*Quito, 1978*)

*I*n Quito, I took the bus to school. Our house was situated near the top of a hill, in a neighborhood appropriately named Bella Vista, for we could see from our windows across the city's apartments and parks to the massive green volcano that is Pichincha. To get to our house near the top of this hill that forms the eastern side of the Andean valley, you had to drive far up a curving street. Our school bus driver was a short, lean man with weathered skin. He was also long-suffering. My siblings and I were invariably late getting ready for the day, and we often heard the roar of the old bus's diesel engine for a good thirty seconds before it ground to a stop in front of our gate. "*¡El bus! ¡El bus!*" we yelled to each other as we scrambled to finish our toast while grabbing book bags and tying shoelaces. I don't know why we said this in Spanish—we usually spoke to each other in English—but we did; it was probably part of our evolving Spanglish lexicon.

The bus driver always waited for us with a patient smile, knowing we would eventually come out at a run to clamber onto the bus. "*Gracias, gracias,*" we panted as we passed him, trying to catch our breath. Once we were all on the bus, my brother and sister and I immediately separated, finding our own friends and classmates and plopping down beside them with a sigh at having made it just in time once again.

The day of the kiss we'd already descended from my house on the hill into the urban valley as we picked up other students on our way to campus. That morning I was staring out the window rather than talking with a schoolmate. Perhaps my friends had stayed home sick from school that day, or had a parent chauffeur them instead of the bus driver. In any case, I was daydreaming as I leaned against the window and gazed at the changing landscape of traffic and shops, pedestrians, *Chiclets* vendors, and bus stops. It was next to one of the latter that my own bus idled at a red light. I looked, without really seeing, at the group of people gathered to wait for their ride. Suddenly my eyes focused on a particular movement, a specific gesture, perhaps a nod of the head. A man stood out from the crowd, holding the hand of a little girl. I noticed him because he was staring at me as I sat in my school bus with the other elementary and middle schoolers. When he saw that he'd caught my eye, his expression slipped into an easy and almost languid lasciviousness. Then, in what seemed to me slow motion, he pursed his lips into a long, and exaggerated, kiss.

I stared back. It was all I could do. I was mesmerized, caught in a spider's sticky web, unable to move. I was just eleven or twelve, and my brain couldn't make sense of a grown man taking note of me, selecting me, a young girl, in this way, especially while holding the hand of an even younger girl. Was this little girl, perhaps five years old, a daughter or a sister or a niece? Because I was so young, I was only dimly aware of Ecuador's "national pastime," the hounding and harassing of women on the streets—sometimes with simple compliments, sometimes with the predatory determination of the *machista*—and there on my school bus, with my books next to me and my classes to look forward to, I'd felt safe. It hadn't occurred to me that I could be a target in that context, and at that age.

This memory is particularly distasteful—I still wince when

I think about it—because I could see, even across a street full of cars and street hawkers, the white flecks of spittle on the man's full lips as they extended toward me, fleshy and moist, his eyes above them knowing in their affront, deliberate in their insult. How many times did this man do this in a month? A week? A day? Looking back as an adult, it seemed automatic on his part and, on those bustling city streets, mundane. But to me then, twelve years old at most, it felt monstrous and perverse, illicit. As the memory plays out in slow motion—the busy morning stilled around me, all engines and voices and horns silenced— that act, that movement, that kiss, hits me like a blow. Yet I didn't say anything to anyone. Only years later did I talk about it, when I'd shaped those few seconds into a funny narrative, a gross joke. That day I kept the sight of that man and his lips to myself, to mull over and ponder, to remember again and again, revolted yet questioning: *Who was that? Why did he do that? Why did he choose me?* I had many questions back then, but no answers— I was still pubescent, still naïve.

Could this have been my first kiss? Of course it wasn't really, yet because of one person's sense of entitlement over another's perception, over the way she will feel and what she will think about and what she will fear during her day and her week and into her future, because of a man's callous indifference to the texture and flavor of the memories that will shape a girl's child-hood, that man's pursed mouth, the wet flecks, the dissonance of the obscene kiss juxtaposed against the little girl clutching his hand, will always be with me, for life. In a small way, clearly— yet it's there, a presence forever, as long as my memory serves me, or even longer. For who can measure how one event, even among countless others, helps mold a person, their personality, their very essence?

León

(Quito, 1979)

I once had a friend called Angela León. I've always liked the last name *León*, translating as it does from the Spanish *león* to the English "lion." It seems to me at once strong, elegant, and not too long, forceful with its two syllables and powerful in meaning.

Angela León and I weren't great friends, which is to say she wasn't part of my inner circle. I had a sort of club of very close friends, one that was inclusive until we felt we had enough vetted members, at which point we became, as is common with young girls, fiercely and self-consciously exclusive. More a familiar classmate than a good friend, then, Angela León was definitely not part of my club. I went to her house just once in the four years I lived in Quito. She was in my grade in our Evangelical middle school, and one of the only Ecuadorians there. Our school was primarily for temporary expats and missionaries, and the only nationals admitted at that time were those who had at least one international parent. I assume this was the case with Angela León, although I don't recall what her parents looked like or what their first names were, because, besides being flawlessly bilingual in Spanish and English, she had light brown hair and intense blue eyes. Both her hair and her eyelashes, coincidentally, reminded me of manes. Her hair was thick and bushy around her thin white face. She had big eyes that had a mesmerizing effect because of their dense, almost black lashes. They were like a forest of lashes, crowding in tiny bunches around her dark blue eyes.

What stands out to this day about the one sleepover I had at Angela León's house was the marathon talk we had in her bedroom before we finally fell asleep in the early morning on top of the bedcovers, still fully clothed, without having brushed our teeth or washed our faces. But before that we spent some time outside, in her garden, and I do remember it was full of green—trees and shrubs, vines and leaves—like a jungle, almost, or, as my mother would have put it, *casi como una selva*. Still, there must have been some order to the chaos, because they had a gardener. In South American countries like Ecuador, and in cities like Quito, it was common for households in certain neighborhoods to have a gardener or even two who came from morning till night to tend the plants and lawns every day, six days a week.

This garden, lush and overgrown as it remains in my memory, also had a fence. I know it was there because Angela León told me about it. She told me about playing outside, in her garden, on her own. Was she an only child? She might have been—there are no siblings in my recollection of that night at her house. When she played in that jungly garden by herself, she sometimes wished to go over this fence. But the problem was that it was too tall for her and she couldn't do it on her own. This is when, as she told me that night in her room, the gardener would appear. Apparently, anytime she approached this fence, the gardener appeared behind her. "*¿Quiere usted ayuda?*" he must have asked, using the formal "*usted*" rather than the informal "*tú*." Or did he use the informal "*tú*" because she was, at eleven or twelve years old, so much younger than him? Perhaps he said, "*Espera un momento, yo te ayudo.*" All I know for sure is what she told me: that he appeared behind her, like an unbidden genie, to help her climb the high fence. He helped her by placing his hand in between her legs so that it cupped her crotch, and then—every time—squeezing as he lifted and guided her over.

She told me this in a shy kind of way, not looking at me, her voice quiet. I don't know how I responded. Did I say, *That's gross*? Or, *That's kind of weird*? Did I ask what it felt like? Did I say anything at all? Maybe I just listened, imagining as she talked this gardener letting go of a shovel or mower dirty with yard debris to reach his arm under her from behind and put his hand over that most private part of her body. This was foreign territory to me, an alien territory where a man—a relatively strange man, one who had been defined to me as belonging to a different class, the servant class, and therefore unknowable—had intimately touched a young girl, my friend.

Two feelings dominate my memory of that one sleepover and even of that particular friend. One is the freedom of talking into the night alone in her room, of bonding over school and gossip and the cute boys in our grade, independent of parents and bedtime routines. We laughed together, intoxicated by our newfound intimacy, flush with that feeling of recognizing the self in the other, of finding the same things funny or sad or titillating. There was a wildness about that freedom, at least for me—it felt strange and rebellious to flout the civilized habits inculcated into me for years by my parents. At home I couldn't imagine going to bed before brushing my teeth, or in anything besides a pair of clean pajamas. But then the darkness, the shadow narrative, imposes itself on my memory and I see again a stain, a mark that impressed itself upon me as I listened to my friend's confession all those years ago.

Angela León never told her parents about the fence and the gardener. I never told my mother or father about them either. I thought of my friend's story as a secret to keep rather than a tale to tell. I went home the next day with my wrinkly clothes and mossy teeth, and when my mother asked "*¿Cómo te fue?*" replied only, "Fine." Why was that? Did Angela León and I feel the same sense of shame? Of discomfort? Of vague unease with speaking what had always been unspoken? We accepted the sense of shame, of blame, as ours, and thus protected the perpetrator with our silence.

I never saw Angela León again outside of school. Our single lasting bond was one of keeping a secret. Life went on for me as part of my club of friends—meeting at the campus courtyard for lunch, calling each other after school to discuss homework or plans for the next day, attending elaborate sleepovers where we dressed up in the host mother's clothes and performed skits that were hysterically funny only to us. I left Angela León behind to her own inner circle of friends, and to a secret that I helped her keep. As a mother and an aunt today, I despair at my complicity in my friend's molestation; I cannot understand why I kept silent. But back then, so many years ago, as a daughter, a young girl, a middle school friend, I didn't think there was another option.

Lolita

(*Quito, 1979*)

*W*as it the pigtails that called to him? The pink plastic balls that held soft blondish hair on either side of the head, the pale part down the middle of the scalp from a childish brow to the exposed nape of a tender neck?

An artist has said that the eye you see is not an eye because you see it, it is an eye because it sees you.

One Sunday when we were living in Ecuador, my family was invited to lunch at the home of a man and his wife who were strangers to everyone but my father. The man was his colleague, and although technically not his boss, a superior nevertheless. I'll always wonder if this hierarchy played into my parents' reaction to our host's behavior that day. I'll never know, though, as I cannot ask — the question is too inappropriate, the answer buried too deep in the past and in the subconscious. The lunch is a memory that was barely kept alive for a few years, simmering on a back burner, by my mother, who used to bring it up now and again. It bothered her that the man, our host, had paid so much attention to my little sister. And then there surfaced a photograph some time ago that served to further shape my own vague memory, until the day itself came into focus and I remembered with clarity my peripheral role in the small, disturbing drama that took place.

I've read that the eyes are the predator's first weapon.

We all went that day—my parents, my little brother, my sister, and I—to this couple's home about twenty minutes from our own. To do so, we had to descend from our house perched high on the slope of Bella Vista, the hill that made up the eastern side of Quito. Imagine a small city, white-washed, itself perched almost ten thousand feet high among the Andes. In this city our house was on a terraced hillside, a long, curvy street up from the valley basin. From our vantage point we were eye-to-eye, so to speak, with the top of Pichincha, the volcano facing us across the valley from the west. We were also at eye level with the planes that made their descent from the south past our house to the airport located in the north; if the passengers had chosen to, they could have waved to us as they flew by the large windows of our living room.

We had to drive down that day into the valley, through more suburban neighborhoods, and past the main park and the one shopping mall to arrive at the more crowded, urban section of the city. We drove until we were under the shadow of El Panecillo, the southern hill where stood the forty-five-meter statue of the Virgin Mary. This was not the Mary I was most familiar with—the gentle, quiet woman, the virgin chosen by God to bear his child. Instead, this was the Mary who vanquished Satan, who crushed, with her bare feet, the head of the serpent she held fast with an iron chain. It was under her figure that we found the apartment we'd been seeking.

From a picture discovered many years later in an old shoebox, I know that once inside the apartment I sat in a corner, on a stiff dining room chair, reading the fat paperback copy of *Gone With the Wind* my mother had bought for me at the supermarket. I occupied the physical periphery of the space, and also the social, because despite the bright dress I wore no one paid any attention to me—least of all the host, who concentrated almost solely on my sister. In this drama I was not even off-stage but rather part of the audience, observer rather than actor.

The photographer as hunter wields his camera as a weapon in the capture of his subject.

In those days, when I was eleven-ish, which made my sister seven-ish, she was the pretty one and I the plain. Family narratives tend to replicate themselves, and back then my sister and I played out our mother's sororal history, in which she grew up as the quiet background to her sister's brilliance. My mother constantly sought to transform me, her ugly duckling, into an acceptable swan, or at least into a more beautiful duck, and she had tried with my outfit: a brightly striped halter dress, modish for the seventies. Yet even the bright stripes, a rainbow of yellow and orange and red, failed to move me out of the shadows and into the spotlight.

In those days it was a lost cause; it would take time to soften some of the glaring irregularities in my physique that contrasted so with my sister's delicate prettiness. As I approached puberty, my hair mutated from manageable waves to untamable curls, and my mother only saw the unruliness that signaled disorder, vulgarity, a degraded version of the smooth-haired blondes who ruled the world. She herself had already spent decades straightening her hair at home in the US with huge rollers, or in Ecuador by going to the salon and having it washed and styled into a silky bob. That day, as I know from the snapshot, my mother had tried to make me look presentable by scraping my hair back from my forehead into a half ponytail. It was slicked close to my scalp and pulled tight, so much so that the hair left loose to fall on my shoulders sprang out, pyramid-like, around my face.

Then there were my big ears, which stuck out from the sides of my head. One night, when I was six and we lived in Manila, I cut my forehead on the bathtub faucet trying to rinse my hair. There was confusion—water, metal, red. My mother took me to the local hospital despite the fact that at that time in the Philippines martial law prohibited travel after dark, under threat of being shot on sight. I found out after I had my wound stitched up, after I went home, and after the scar faded, that the doctor had offered to pin back my ears at the same time he stitched together my cut. A plastic surgeon, he homed in on my elephantine ears the instant he saw me. My mother was tempted, but then thought better of it, trusting that my head would eventually grow into them.

Adding to the overall effect of unappealing pubescence were my front teeth. I had large buck teeth, with a sizeable gap between them. I may or may not have had braces by that particular Sunday luncheon at my father's colleague's apartment. My mother, in her endless quest to make me more palatable to the eye, prettier, less awkward-looking, took me to two different orthodontists. The first couldn't have been very good, for he would have slapped braces on my teeth the very day of our first appointment if my mother had let him. Instead, she took me to get a second opinion, and this orthodontist discovered that I needed a procedure before attaching braces, or else the gap between my two front teeth would never close. As it was, I would spend six years in complicated orthodontia before my teeth straightened for good.

In some cultures, people object to tourists pointing cameras at them and snapping pictures to be consumed later. They fear the soul's abduction, or the theft of some fundamental essence. At the very least, it is an invasion of privacy.

Who knows, though, it could be that even if I'd had small straight teeth, silky-smooth hair, dainty ears, and petite limbs like my sister, I would still have been invisible to this host of ours. Perhaps my eleven-year-old self was too old for a man like him, too close to the grotesque threat that is full, voluptuous womanhood. Perhaps his version of Lolita was more my sister, fairer, younger, and thus, he hoped, more pliable. Neither one of us was the nymphet of Humbert Humbert's fantasies.

My sister had something I can't adequately put into words even now, as an adult, because it is by definition off the charts of my comprehension. But for this man, my sister had the "It" factor. He fixated on her like a raptor as soon as we walked in— eagle-eyed, he recognized her and stalked her for the rest of our time there. It was one continuous plunge, and he caught her with a camera instead of beak or talons.

My sister gave the impression of sweetness and yielding. She was pretty, like a doll. I must have seemed unyielding to a man like him, hard, all angles and knobs in my too-tall-too-soon pubescence. Although I was closer in age to Nabokov's nymphet, this man, our host, barely glanced at me. I didn't matter; I was invisible. True, I was awkward and skinny and ugly—I certainly didn't have nymphet qualities. But neither did my sister. She was too young, I think now, too babyish in her face and limbs. But at that age, who was I to judge a pedophile's taste? I only know today, after college literature classes, for example, the nature of Humbert Humbert's obsession with the young Dolores.

What I did know that day, I could see. And what I saw was a man, old like my father, who for some period of time during our stay that afternoon in his apartment, whether five minutes or twenty, had a camera in his hands pointed exclusively at my sister. She attracted him, she entranced him—it was clear from his exclamations about her sweetness, her loveliness, her pretti-ness. He asked her to pose so that he could take specific shots and she obliged, too young to sense anything untoward in his attention. He was like a man possessed, possessed by a vibrating excitement. I can't help but think it must have been the era— about fifty years ago, a half-century—that allowed his behavior to pass without comment by any of the adults nearby.

A photographer can feel he has ownership not only over an individual subject but also over an entire experience.

Before we left, this man asked if my sister could come and visit again . . . by herself. I don't remember what my mother, or my father for that matter, said at that moment. I remember his asking, not their answering. This man was our host, my father's work superior, but after we left and the door shut behind us, when we were safe in our car, I remember my mother commenting on the strangeness of our host's behavior, and of his request. A mother hen, protective always, she would never have allowed my sister to be alone in such a man's presence. So protective a mother was she that later, when my sons were very young, she advised me not to leave them alone with any boy or man besides their father—cousin, uncle, or neighbor, it didn't matter. They all represented threats.

My husband has talked recently of quantum physics, and how this science posits an infinite number of parallel universes, with alternate realities. In another universe, in another reality, is my mother naïve and ignorant? Does she drop my sister off one afternoon, without even checking if the man's wife is home? Would my parents let their host's superior position in my father's company influence their reactions, even if only subconsciously, and allow this man private access to my sister? It frightens me to think of what this small deviation in reality would have led to: my sister alone and defenseless with a predator.

One night at a New Year's Eve party with my mother, I watched as one of her Peruvian friends pulled a camera from her purse to take pictures of the dancing. It was a large camera, the type with a zoom lens. Another woman pointed it out to the others: "*¡Ay—que macho! ¡Miran chicas, que macho es esa camera!*" They laughed together at the imagined virility of the camera's extending lens. I can't remember now if, years before, our host's camera was big and macho. I'm inclined to think of it as such—

menacing, the lens circling my sister until the man wielding it found the best angle, the cleanest approach, from which to strike. But it had to have been a manual camera, as we were in the late seventies, and I suspect it was also a small, compact one. But, even as such, it would have been equally effective in capturing a likeness, a persona, a fantasy.

If the camera is a bird of prey, still its talons are like a crow's rather than a hawk's. Blunt, so as not to puncture. Curved, so as to catch and then hold fast.

In my mind, similar to the one picture we have of that day, it is my sister and me. I'm in my corner, wearing my stripes, holding my thick paperback with the cover matching my dress, bright in reds and oranges as Atlanta burns behind Scarlet and Rhett. My sister is more central, standing up in her sweet blue dress with the white smocking and puffed sleeves. She is smiling—not a broad, confident smile, not a coy, flirty smile, but an innocent, seven-year-old smile. At the time, I didn't see her as so very young; we were sisters, after all, and I was but eleven. Now, as an adult, eleven seems much older than seven. As children however, we were close enough in age for me to compare us in that competitive sibling way. And I always lost when it came to looks.

The day of the luncheon, the man's constant hovering over my sister, his obvious adulation, his continuously pointed lens, were proof once again that I had failed. I had failed at living up to an ideal. But it wasn't jealousy I felt then—I didn't want, after all, to be seven again, or wear a smocked dress, or have pigtails shaped into ringlets by our mother—it was disappointment. I sensed that I had failed my mother's expectations, that I reminded her of herself in comparison to her own sister. How she was the darker, plainer one, and her sister the cosseted beauty in the spotlight of everyone's attention.

Although young, I had a clear sense of myself and how I

didn't fulfill my own expectations for how I should look—the ideal way a girl is supposed to look when practicing femininity. In my bedroom I had a triptych mirror on a vanity, my mother's before mine, smooth wood curving around the top of each panel. I used to sit at this vanity and stare at my own reflection from three different angles, willing my face to somehow become— magically, miraculously—prettier. The skin lighter, the eyes bigger, the ears smaller, the teeth even, the hair, always the hair, smoother, silkier, straighter. Of course that never happened, but I know I went through this exercise in insecurity because at least once I had an out-of-body experience in which I watched myself doing what I was doing. Looking at myself in the mirrors, hoping that from a certain angle I might look pretty. Our host with the camera that day was like the mirror's reflection, showing me that I wasn't at all attractive or desirable.

Once I begged my mother to try blowing my hair dry at home rather than at the salon, where I dreaded the pain from the detangling by the stylist's narrow-toothed comb. My mother did what I asked (she never denied me anything), although it was clear she didn't have high hopes. Standing beside me as I sat on the edge of the tub in the bathroom, she brushed my hair while pointing the nozzle of the dryer at my head. The outcome was far from satisfying. Looking at the result in the mirror, I thought I might cry: my hair had expanded into a huge triangle, each individual strand defiant and kinky. I went to bed bitterly disappointed. From the darkness of my room a few minutes later I was aware of my mother entering the guest room where my grandmother was staying for a few weeks. I overheard my grandmother ask, "*¿Cómo se ve?*" and my mother sigh, "*Horroroso.*"

The camera as gaze is an instrument of power.

What did he do, this man, with the photos? Did he rush to pick them up from the developers a couple of days after he dropped them off, so anxious was he to hold them, view them, own them? Did he add these photographs to the growing stash hidden in a secret drawer to choose from when alone, free at last to cater to his most private desires?

In the days I'm referencing, not only was I eleven but the time period was the 1970s, when certain topics were not talked about, when certain identities were never acknowledged. I did not know the word *pedophile*. I didn't even know the words *child molester* or *pervert*. Yet I saw how this man coveted my sister, and I felt rather than thought the ideas of *predator, hunting, stalking*. So even as I was disappointed in my own undesirability, in my invisibility in the corner with my fluffy hair and dark face and buck teeth, I also have, now, a sense of ominousness saturating my memory, hanging over my family and permeating the afternoon.

So if some of this sounds like I wished I'd received the same kind of attention my sister received from this man, I don't think that is the case. I sensed something sinister about our host and his seeming obsession with a seven-year-old girl. I didn't want the stalking and the capture. I didn't want the beating of wings about my head, the leathery talons on my skin, their rough clasp around my body. But I did want the gaze. I wanted to feel like someone was looking at me in this time of life when I was rehearsing for womanhood, waiting for the audition but not knowing when to expect it. And I needed to have this someone look at me with approval. I dreaded what I felt that day—the rejection implied by the lack of attention, by the look never attracted, the gaze never given.

The trigger for that man, our host, may have been the pigtails, long and glossy, curled smoothly in ringlets fastened at the top with the pink plastic balls. I'll never know. No one can know, except the man himself. Then there's the wife, the missing character in this drama. He had one; we all met her that day. Where was she when her husband followed my sister, this young pigtailed girl, around the living room and into the dining room, wielding his camera as if talons outstretched? I have no recollection of her presence when we were leaving and her husband asked for my sister to be dropped off with him someday soon, let alone any memory of anything she may have said. She is the truly invisible, the most overlooked, in my memory of that long-ago day.

It's been said that the photographing eye is insatiable. Probably, too, is the pedophile's.

No one can know what the host did with the film in his camera. But I can speculate. Maybe he chose to develop the photographs himself in order to experiment with them, wanting more direct control, more tactile participation in their creation. Perhaps he played with superimposition, placing onto my sister different images, or with tone, lightening and darkening various features, or with color, brightening and muting aspects of her likeness. Perhaps he fancied himself a modern-day Pygmalion and, with the image of a living breathing girl, using darkroom materials, fashioned for himself his own ideal Lolita.

Breasts

(Quito, 1980)

I 'd never seen my mother's breasts. Or anyone else's, for that matter. I didn't have an older sister to learn from, and at twelve — I was a late bloomer — my own were just beginning to develop. All of which explains why I was staring with such intensity at those breasts, naked and pale, in front of me.

Despite the impression her breasts made on me, I don't remember her name. But the vague idea of her I still have tells me she was an R person. I'll call her Racquel, a name suitably sophisticated for the girl, older than me, whose developed breasts were the first I was able to study at some length, in real life. I say at some length, but since she was merely changing her clothes rather than posing for my benefit, my time with her breasts was probably half a minute at most. Yet I was greedy, and the sight of those naked breasts mesmerized me. I couldn't turn my eyes away. Part of me felt awkward because I knew it was inappropriate and weird for me to be staring at her body, but still my ignorance goaded me to take in as much as possible, to learn, to know. Was I looking at my own future?

My memory places me with Racquel in the master bedroom of my family's expatriate home in Quito, the bedroom shared by my mother and father. We are both standing, Racquel and I, and she is changing clothes. I remember her talking while I listen and stare, trying to memorize as much as I can of her breasts in the short time I have. Racquel has red hair and her breasts are pale like milk. Already I know that my chest will never look like hers. My skin is much darker, a dense olive rather than a translucent ivory. Her skin is so fair that I can see the faint blue of veins threading throughout her chest and down her breasts. They look impossibly large to me, but in hindsight, years after my own maturation, I realize they probably filled a B cup at most. The nipples are pink and seem mysterious and foreign yet, at the same time, utterly in keeping with the soft roundness of the flesh that shifts gently with the movement of Racquel's arms.

During those same few moments, forever crystallized in my imagination as a pair of milky-white breasts traced softly with blue, we are talking about religion. I don't know where Racquel came from; she wasn't in my grade, perhaps she didn't even attend my school, and yet there she was, in my house—my friend, my mentor, my crush. Most likely she was the daughter of one of my mother's friends. She probably attended the secular American school in the city. I must have told her that day about my religion—not about my inherited Catholicism but about my adopted belief system, the one taught at my Evangelical school. Ever the earnest student, I'd internalized its precepts, like fairy tales in their simplicity, relatively quickly. Thus I must have mentioned Jesus and his role as "Our Personal Savior," proclaimed the need to have faith in Christ as "The way and the truth and the light," and insisted on "born again" status as the one-way ticket to Heaven.

Even then, still on the cusp of puberty, I noticed her calm demeanor, the mature way she explained her own, different set of beliefs. "In my religion," she said, "we believe in reincarnation."

Reincarnation? To me it was a new word, long and strange and threatening.

Racquel must have sensed my confusion, maybe even my fear, because she continued, mildly but with conviction, "I believe that after I die I'll come back. My spirit will come back, in another body."

Memory shows me standing there, doing nothing but gazing at my friend's naked breasts, while also trying to make sense of what she was saying. The idea of reincarnation was so alien to me that I found it distressing; I couldn't grasp its implications. It seemed to me evil in its opposition to everything I'd had normalized by the missionary teachers as right and natural and good. *Come back . . . as someone else? Have another*—different—*mother and father, sister and brother? No . . . Impossible! This can't be true!*

I must have stammered my incredulity, my protestations against this bizarre idea, but I don't recall exactly in what words. I do know that the next time she came to my house Racquel said, "Let's not talk about religion anymore. I know it makes you sad."

There is another vision of breasts that has stayed with me throughout the decades since my adolescence. In this image, the breasts are covered, yet I can see their shape and size, and even the darker shade of their nipples. These breasts are baptized breasts. During my middle school years, years I spent in Quito, I attended at least one baptism. The Christians of my missionary school believed not in the mild, sprinkly type of baptism—the Catholic version where the priest gathers family and friends, parents and godparents, around the baptismal font—but in the full-immersion type where ministers bring the members of the parish with those ready to be baptized around a pool or tub. In this version, the baptismal candidate must have reached the age of reason and therefore be able to choose baptism freely, to choose complete immersion, clothed in white, by a minister into the body of water arranged for this purpose.

There was a lot of people at that baptism—men, women, and children, all of them faithful congregants. The air was warm and the water cold. I was never part of these rituals myself, being the daughter of an atheist father as well as a Catholic mother who couldn't have been more disinterested in the odd, overly serious traditions of this Anglo-Evangelical group. I knew the water was cold because of the gasps that came involuntarily from the newly baptized as they were lifted up, soaking wet, by the officiating preacher. I also knew because of the raised nipples of the girls and women who, smiling shyly and automatically trying to cover their chests, walked out of the water amid cheering and applause.

There's a reason I never saw my mother's breasts. My mother attended a boarding school in Lima during her adolescence. There the nuns taught the girls to ask for permission to go to the "Little Room" rather than the "bathroom" or "toilet." Covered in stiff layers that hid any feminine curve like armor, the Catholic sisters taught shame around the body. To this day, my mother changes for bed under the voluminous tent of her nightgown. As she was instructed at the Sagrado Corazón, she pulls her nightgown over her head; then, protected by curtains of material from any gaze, even her own, she carefully removes her clothes. When I was younger, I thought this a neat trick. Now I see it as another of patriarchy's scams, one in which women are taught to be ashamed of their own bodies, to hide them unless purposely displayed for the male gaze.

A few years after attending the baptism, I receive a very different impression of the female body from that of my mother hiding behind a thick veil of material. I am in Peru with my family, visiting my aunt and uncle and cousins. I walk by a bathroom door that's open just a crack, enough for me to glimpse movement behind it. I stop to peer through the narrow sliver of space between door and frame, not thinking about spying or any invasion of privacy—instead, merely curious, I act instinctively. What I see is my aunt, just out of the shower, reflected in the large mirror over the sink. She is looking into the same mirror while drying her back. Pulling the towel back and forth behind her, she gazes at her reflection, and the look on her face is one of pride. At this point, middle-aged, she has given birth to seven full-term babies. Her body is not perfect—there's a soft belly instead of a taut abdomen, slack instead of muscled thighs, breasts that have begun to droop, small and well-used. Yet I see her; I serve as a witness: she admires her own nakedness. As a young girl she attended the same school as my mother; the two sisters wore the same uniform, slept in the same dormitory, practiced piano in the same dark, cavernous gym. Where did this assurance come from?

In contrast to my aunt's private pride, there was something vulnerable about those girls and women, those converts to blind faith whom I saw baptized so many years ago, that has stayed with me. Pleased to be there, to have officially been made part of the group, to have been embraced by a select community, they also seemed eager to please. The wet, white material clung to their bodies, outlining every crease and curve, every roll, wrinkle, hip bone, and goose bump, making pathetically ineffective their efforts at shielding themselves with their hands, at defending themselves from the men who stared at them even as they praised God, thanked the Lord, and welcomed these women and their baptized bodies into the Holy Church.

Forever these two differing impressions of breasts, for some the absolute quintessence of femininity, will war in the memories of my youth: Racquel's self-assurance as she changes in front of me, and the feelings of indignity that, along with the transparent material, covered the bodies of the Christian women. It's still a tangle for me, and I continue to comb through the threads of my perception of the past, pulling them apart to find out how they intertwined and caught—what, looking back, snagged and twisted. I see how the baptized girls and women were laid bare, not from a covering of cloth but from dignity and privacy and self-possession. And how, in contrast, Racquel's breasts remain free in my imagination from any sense of mortification or shame. Instead I remember their nakedness—their pallor, their curves, the soft vulnerability of their flesh and its outline of veins—through the prism of Racquel herself, her quiet conviction, her understanding, her kindness.

Flawed Fairy Tale

(Lima, 1982)

We lounge about in my grandmother's house in Miraflores, one of Lima's residential neighborhoods. It's that in-between time of day when you're a child on vacation visiting relatives, with no structure to your hours, no school or homework or chores. Lunch has been eaten, dinner is still hours away, the afternoon stretches before us. My little brother and sister and I sprawl on the couch or in armchairs with two of our young cousins. At fourteen, I am the oldest of the group. Some of us read a book, others watch TV, all of us are idle. My grandmother, mother, and aunt chat, as they always do, engaging in what seems to me a running stream of endless gossip.

This house, the one my grandmother owns, is used both as an office for her son-in-law and grandsons and as a meeting place for family and friends and employees who pass by throughout the day. Although the house is located in one of the "better" neighborhoods, it's still protected from intruders by an iron cage that encloses the entrance. To access the house, you need two keys: one for the metal gate, one for the front door. On this particular day, one I remember as hot and lazy and long, the bell at the gate interrupts our lounging with a harsh buzz. Bored and ready for distraction, we children jump to look out the window and see who it is; one of us opens the door and peeks out.

There stands a young woman. To me, an ungainly teen with buck teeth and braces, frizzy hair and pimples, she seems impossibly sophisticated in her tiny bikini top and frayed denim mini-skirt, manicured toes on rubber flip-flops, blonde hair bleached blonder by the sun, fair skin bronzed from days lingering on the beach.

"*¡Hola!*" she calls from the sidewalk, beyond the black bars. "*Soy Leticia. Vengo por Carlos — ¿está adentro?*"

"Carlos! Carlos! She wants Carlos!"

Carlos, one of my older cousins, walks into the room from the back stairwell and takes in the scene. Annoyed, he tells us to quit staring and get away from the window; then, frowning with irritation, he strides past us toward the door and the pretty young woman beyond it.

Carlos's annoyance at our attention to his visitor, I know now, comes from the fact that he is married to someone else. His wife Kelly is also blonde, although her skin is fairer, less tanned. She is petite and elegant and educated. Because her parents are expats from the United States, she speaks both English and Spanish perfectly. Older than Carlos, she married him when she became pregnant with their first child.

This day, I struggle to make sense of what has transpired. What have I just seen? I intuit, somehow, that there's something illicit about my cousin, my married cousin, leaving abruptly with someone not his wife, another blonde, another pretty, petite woman. His irritation with us—the witnesses to his guilt—adds to my perception of a clandestine quality to her appearance and his departure, to my sense of something furtive about the speed with which he exited the house, without looking back.

All the knowledge I'm able to gather comes from my observations and the snatches of conversation I glean from my mother and aunt and grandmother. Yes, Carlos is seeing someone. In the euphemistic language of a patriarchal culture where women are dispensable and men are prized, in the softened tones of a loving aunt, mother, and grandmother, words like "cheating," "infidelity," and "adultery" are never spoken aloud, in English or in Spanish. Instead there are phrases like *"pobrecita la Kelly,"* and *"que está pensando Carlos, la Kelly es tan fina,"* and *"esto no va a durar, él sólo está jugando con la otra."* Any sense of outrage seems concentrated on the differences between Kelly and Leticia: Kelly is *"fina"*—she has a degree from UC Santa Barbara, and holds herself with a distinct air of refinement. She is a wife and a mother who expects a certain gravitas from her husband and the father of her child. Leticia is, as my aunt later dubs her in her accented English, "wash and wear." More casual and less proper, she promises fun and spontaneity. Over the years, the narrative will shift from "poor Kelly" and "what is he thinking" to "well what do you expect, she's older than him" and "that's what you get for seducing a man." There's no mercy, even from the sisterhood, for another woman betrayed by a beloved son, nephew, grandson.

This moment in time, this scene from my childhood, hazy and vague in outline but keen and palpable in emotion, embodies much of what, growing up, I struggled to understand, to make sense of, to align with my youthful, fairy-tale morality. How to make agree a narrative of *till death do us part* in front of a priest or a judge, dressed in silk and white lace, a narrative that includes parents as well as an aunt and uncle who are still together, who do not engage in adulterous love stories, with the narrative unfolding before me, in real time, one that speaks of faithlessness and deception, lying and cheating? How to match the narrative of respect and admiration for Kelly, the wife of my cousin, the classy addition to our extended family, the princess to my cousin's Prince Charming, with that of Leticia, this newcomer, this interloper, this coauthor, ultimately, of tragedy for the legal partner, the legitimate love, the wife?

I grew up worshiping my Peruvian cousins and their glamorous lifestyle—the long days at the beach, the familiarity with the sun and the waves, the ease with which they inhabited their place in life, the imperturbable self-assurance, the confidence, the cool. I came from a place of painful self-consciousness, of acute awareness of my flaws and limitations: too tall, too skinny, too dark, too serious, too earnest. I came from a place of black-and-white values: you either lied or you told the truth, stepped up or shirked responsibility, were faithful or unfaithful, constant or inconstant, monogamous or adulterous.

After their hurried wedding one summer several years prior to the afternoon when Leticia came calling on my cousin, Carlos and Kelly briefly stayed with my family in Northern California as part of a honeymoon trip up and down the coast. She was still not showing, still petite, with a poise that evoked care rather than fastidiousness, quiet self-possession rather than showy sophistication. He was the cool Peruvian cousin, looking like a young Richard Gere or the lead in a telenovela, with skin brown from the sun, chest lean and arms muscled from surfing. I remember sitting and staring, trying to absorb their allure, their attraction. I wanted that for myself but felt irrevocably removed from it as if by the height and heft of an impassable barrier—a wall unyieldingly rooted, fast and firm. I could see through it but not reach across it; it was impossible to share in their charm, to claim even a portion of their charisma as my own. They seemed to exist on a plane separate from my own, an inaccessible planet where life was a mixture of beauty and romance, ease and luxury. Who was I in comparison?

We lived then in a small cottage in a part of California known more for icy, shark-infested waters than warm, bikini-covered beaches. At home we rarely went to restaurants; in Lima my cousins routinely ate out, often at ritzy clubs, country or beach, where it was customary to lie by a pool and order drinks from uniformed staff. I had chores—daily dishes, weekly vacuuming, monthly cupboard airing. My cousins grew up with servants—cooks and maids and gardeners—who prepared meals of arroz con pollo, served ice-cold glasses of limeade when it was hot outside, mowed the lawn and watered the ferns, or made the beds while their employers breakfasted on bread rolls, sliced ham, and sweet, milky Nescafé.

That day, the day Leticia showed up at the door, the day we sat idle and bored and ready for distraction, Kelly was nowhere to be seen. I didn't know where she was; I knew only that she wasn't with us at my grandmother's house, at the makeshift office also used as a meeting place for the extended family. Most probably she was at her own house, the one she shared with Carlos. What's certain is that Kelly was off-stage that afternoon and in her place was Leticia. Leticia, also pretty and blonde and petite; Leticia the stranger, mysterious and unknown; Leticia, moving onto center-stage. What could I make of this new protagonist in the ongoing saga of my Peruvian family? How could I make sense of this new narrative? How could I make conform the new and the old, the strange and the familiar, the unspoken and the official? At the time, I was only vaguely aware of the implications, intuiting, fuzzily and imprecisely, the hurt and humiliation Kelly must have felt. I felt pressured to share the lens of my mother, aunt, and grandmother, and adopt the perspective of my cousin Carlos, who, as the young, handsome husband— entitled, fun-loving, and charming—could hardly be expected to stay faithful to one woman.

I did learn what happened in the end; I learned the temporary resolution to this particular drama, the conclusion to one of the chapters in the story of my cousin and his wife. I found out what happened, once again, from listening in the backseats of cars, at the ends of dining tables, from my perch adjacent to couches where women sat conversing, discussing, analyzing.

Carlos bought a heavy gold Rolex, a potent symbol of wealth and status in 1980s Lima, and, seemingly contrite, presented it to Kelly as a gift that was both apology and bribe. It may have worked that one time but in the end, in the real end, *en el fin*, she divorced him—left Carlos, exited our family, rejected the flawed fairy tale to make her own life far away in snowy Michigan. Although in some ways I betray my family by thinking so disloyally, I feel a sense of satisfaction with this conclusion. In the end, she could not be bought.

The Pinch

(*Quito, 1983*)

I sit in the living room of Sarah's house in Quito on a Sunday morning. I am fifteen. Only last summer, my family returned to California after four years in Ecuador. I missed both the city and my friend so much that I've flown back for a three-week visit.

Sarah and I became fast friends at the Evangelical missionary school we attended, despite neither one of us being Evangelical; it happened to be the best American school in the city, according to my parents and hers, with the kindest and gentlest campus culture.

This Sunday, a handful of families has come to join Sarah's for a Church of Christ service. All expatriates from the States, they line up on the sofa, settle in the armchairs, or claim one of the extra seats brought in for the meeting. Small children play in a separate room with Sarah's younger sister as babysitter.

During the service, I notice that although Sarah's brother, just two years older than us, is asked to lead the singing, Sarah is not. My friend has explained to me in past conversations about religion that because the human voice alone is "pleasing to God," her church doesn't worship with instruments. In the several years Sarah and I have been close, I've learned that members of the Church of Christ take the Bible literally. Because singing hymns is expressly encouraged while there is a "silence in the Scriptures" about playing instruments, Sarah's family supports the prohibition of instrumental music in church. This morning I wonder why my friend, unlike her brother, has no role in the service.

Although I'm tempted, I never find the right moment to lean toward her as she sits beside me and whisper, "Why aren't you ever asked to lead the singing?"

Instead I do what I always do when I'm bored: study the people around me. One of the mothers appears to be in her mid-twenties. Her face, heart-shaped and delicate, is quietly, remarkably, beautiful. Always drawn to beauty, I observe this young mother for a long time. Her long skirt and plain cotton shirt highlight her features. A pale blonde, she wears her hair in an old-fashioned style with a center part above her wide brow and two neat braids wrapped around her head. Like a serene Madonna, she seems a figure more suited to a Catholic church, with its smooth stone statues and formal portraits, than to Sarah's modern, practical house with its wide sofas, wall-to-wall-carpet, and brand new Betamax video player. I can't stop staring at this young mother, whose children are in the other room playing while the adults and teenagers worship.

At one point the young Madonna's little boy, about nine years old, emerges from the playroom. He's been banished be-cause of bad behavior. Perhaps he refused to share, or laughed during a Bible story, or shoved his sibling. Joining the rest of the intimate congregation, he sits meekly at his mother's feet, his back to her, knees bent and arms wrapped around his legs, taking up as little space as possible.

The worshipers begin a prayer. It occurs to me that the Protestant prayers familiar to me vary according to the person — always a man — voicing them. Some prayers are short and hur-ried, others long and leisurely. The long ones seem to be about ego, about the praying person listening to himself speak, about gauging how impressive he sounds to his audience. The short ones are about getting through a task in order to get down to the real business, whether a meal, a class, or a meeting. Although I'm sure I heard sincere prayers during my four-year tenure at the missionary school, I mostly recall the glib cadences of a taken-for-granted ritual.

My love of observation extends to prayer and, this morning, my eyes open to witness the sweet-looking mother soundlessly pinching her son's back as he sits on the floor in front of her. Very precisely, through the thin material of his shirt, the young Christian woman uses her thumb and forefinger to exert pressure on her son's skin, squeezing harder and harder until her arm trembles. The small boy hunches over as he hugs his knees, his skinny frame and scrunched-up face tense with the supreme effort of keeping silent. The prayer seems to go on and on, the pinch seems to go on and on, intensifying with each second that passes, with each word uttered.

I am shocked by this silent, maternal violence. Only when I'm much older will I consider the possibility that the beautiful blonde Madonna may have been ashamed that her son misbehaved. She may have believed that this reflected poorly on her—on her parenting, on her image as a Christian mother raising a Christian child. She may have internalized the Old Testament precept of "spare the rod and spoil the child." She may have been hurt herself when young and vulnerable. She may have feared repercussions from her husband for not controlling their son. She may have been taking out her own frustrations, her own feelings of powerlessness—even if unvoiced and unacknowledged—on her child.

This morning, however, all I feel is a repulsion magnified by fear and confusion. That kind of violence, perpetrated by a mother—a quiet, beautiful, Christian mother—is incomprehensible to me.

Still, despite what I've just seen, I remember after the service to ask my friend, "How come you're never called to lead anything like your brother?"

Casually, Sarah replies, "'Cause girls are supposed to be quiet during church."

"What? What're you *talking* about?"

"That's what it says in the Bible."

"Are you *sure*?"

"Yeah, ask my mom."

"I don't believe it." I shake my head. "God wouldn't prefer boys over girls! Where in the Bible?"

"I don't know." Sarah shrugs. "Ask my mom."

At the first opportunity, I approach Sarah's mother in the kitchen and ask her if the Bible really does state that girls should be quiet in church. Sarah nods in an I-told-you-so fashion as her mother, with the self-possession of the righteous, verifies that yes indeed the New Testament prescribes the silencing of women and girls. Still disbelieving, I find the family Bible in the father's study and, after placing it carefully on the desk, open it to the verse Sarah's mother has directed me to: *1 Corinthians 14:34*. Standing opposite the official-looking chair I dare not sit in, I read. And there it is in black and white. Paul writes to the Corinthian congregation:

> As in all the congregations of the saints, women should remain silent in the churches. They are not allowed to speak, but must be in submission . . . If they want to inquire about something, they should ask their own husbands at home; for it is disgraceful for a woman to speak in the church.

Today, as a middle-aged woman, I look back at that moment as a scene in a movie with my young self as the protagonist. I feel sorry for that girl, contemplating her with a kind of sympathetic compassion. I know that as she reads the black words on the white page, all of it—sentences and paragraphs, verses and chapters—bound in thick brown leather, her chest tightens with a kind of desperate disappointment. *Submission? Disgraceful?* Until this moment she has believed in a God who is infinitely wise and whose love is unconditional. She's been *taught* to believe in a God with infinite wisdom and unconditional love. She feels betrayed. God—Loving Father, Divine Force, Omniscient Being—favors men over women, considers boys superior to girls. She stands staring at the printed words in the leather-bound book, heavy with authority, in front of her.

Before leaving, she closes the Bible to hide the words—which have, in effect, struck a damaging blow to her worldview, a worldview she doesn't yet consciously hold as hers. At this point her philosophy of life, with feminism as its guiding principal, is but a stumbling toddler, a first and tentative draft of a poem, the broadly sketched outline of a painting.

This girl, then, the protagonist of my past, is no longer the innocent believer she was when she first entered the office. She walks out knowing she can argue no further with Sarah, or Sarah's mother, or the Church of Christ and its rules about active men and silent women. She has lost, and in more ways than one.

U nlike with the Biblical decree against women speaking in church, I don't remember if I spoke with anyone about the Madonna-like mother and her vicious pinch. I don't know today if I described what I'd seen to my friend, or if Sarah listened to my account with the same degree of shock at a mother's violence, or of bewildered pity for a small son, as I'd had as witness. I do know that these events, occurring at different moments on the same day, remain forever interlocked, connected irrevocably by context and theme. The sound of male voices speaking, praying, leading in song. The silence of the young boy, skinny limbs clenched, at the feet of his sweet-faced mother. Women gagged, muzzled, stifled—by the decrees of Saint Paul. The pent-up rage of the beautiful Madonna, quiet helpmeet to her husband, silent servant within the church, wife and mother so young. The men, again—praying, singing, preaching. The white-knuckled hand, the thin shirt.

Part Two

THE
GROWING
YEARS

The Cadillac

(*California, 1984*)

*W*hat I remember the most from that moment was my right leg stretched over the seat, its foot planted on the concrete drive. I was acutely conscious of that foot outside the car, keeping the passenger door from closing, keeping me from being shut in, imprisoned, with escape becoming difficult or even impossible.

I was in yet another awkward situation, the kind in which I found myself more and more often. I hated those types of interactions and did almost anything to avoid them, but somehow there I was once again. Trapped.

That morning I'd driven to the house of a friend, a musician who played the viola every weekend throughout high school with the San Francisco Youth Orchestra. Such was my boredom, or perhaps my constant yearning for the companionship of my friends, that I'd abandoned my family at home quite happily, without a thought for what my brother, sister, or parents might want from me on a Saturday, and fled to Enika's, where we'd climbed into her family's old VW Bus for the drive from Marin to San Francisco.

Perched on the van's seats, we had an almost panoramic view through its wide windows of the Bridge and the Bay as we talked avidly about all the small things that fascinated us at seventeen: clothes or what hair spray kept our overgrown bangs trendily high or the fact that her mother's old Maybelline eyeliner lasted such a long time throughout the nights of drinking and dancing to New Wave music like the Thompson Twins and Fun Boy Three. We talked about the people we'd see at the clubs—the slim blond boy who always wore giant diamante earrings, the dark-haired girl who danced by herself with her eyes closed, and our friend Laurence with his sailor's cap. We talked about having enough money to buy a pack of Marlboro Lights to smoke at the café with our black coffee before heading back to the city later that night.

Once we arrived at the Davies Symphony Hall, where the youth orchestra's all-day practices were held, we separated— Enika and her banged-up viola case to the stage and I to my pick of audience seats in the empty theater. From that darkened cocoon I could watch the lighted stage. I knew the cast of characters preparing to play because Enika had told me stories about the different boys and girls who made up the orchestra. Who was favored by the conductor, who wasn't. Who was truly nice, and who was nice to one's face but gossiped behind it. Who was a natural talent, who was a hard worker. I always looked for the gangly violinist with the thin brown hair optimistically styled in a Farrah Fawcett flip who, according to Enika, targeted her as a main competitor. What made things worse in our eyes was that this competitive girl would run to the snack table in front of all the others to scoop up the best of the muffins and cookies. We had no compassion for this other girl, her competitive nature only justifying our seeking of any perceptible flaws for which to judge her. In this way Enika and I, in our teenage way, could believe ourselves smarter, trendier, better—at the very least more polite.

The sounds of squeaking chairs, tuning instruments, and turning pages were familiar to me as I watched the students pluck at their strings, draw their bows, and adjust their mouth-pieces. I knew the automatic relaxation of the body of a cellist or drummer after their portion of the score was done for the moment. I noticed the tensing, the sitting up and checking of sheet music of the musicians readying to play. I recognized the boredom in the faces of those who waited for their turn.

After an hour or two sheltered by the dim light of the empty hall, watching my friend and the other students on the stage, I walked outside to the bright light of the late morning. My mission was always the same: get lunch. I had to find a place that sold cheap but appetizing food, like chips and a sandwich, to bring back in time for my friend's break. I often took this opportunity to look around me and observe the different activities of the city I wasn't always privy to, living as I did in what I considered the boring suburbs across the Golden Gate.

On this particular morning I was still walking on Van Ness, the broad boulevard that links the north side of the city to the south, when a car stopped me mid-path. A big black Cadillac pulled into an alley that divided the sidewalk, forcing me to step back. The passenger window rolled down and the driver, a man, leaned over the empty seat toward me.

"Hello, beautiful girl," he said, in an accent unusual to me. "I want to talk with you. Come inside here, come sit down."

How did I go from hearing this invitation from a strange man who had just swerved from traffic and pulled in front of my path to sitting in his car? *I was seventeen, for God's sake*, I think to myself now. *Not seven.* I do know the answer, though. And it's a sad tale of daily indoctrination: don't hurt people's feelings, don't make a scene, and avoid embarrassment at all costs, even that created by another.

I do remember some weak remonstration on my part — asking him, "Why do I need to get in the car? Why can't you just tell me through the window?" But he only responded, in his somewhat formal English, "Nothing is wrong. Why are you so frightened? I would like to talk with you."

I let myself be convinced. Why? Because I wanted to spare his feelings, because the idea of a firm *No* on my part, of a sudden turning-away, was fraught with mortification, and part of me (apparently the dominant part) simply could not do it. So, instead of obeying the rules I'd been taught by my mother, I obeyed a strange man.

Not because it makes the fact that I got into a car driven by a stranger any more or less dangerous but because it adds to my later understanding of the situation and its unique characteristics, I will point out that the man in the car wore what I later learned was a galabiya, as well as a headdress I recognized even then as typical of Saudi Arabian men. His body was clothed in a long white robe-coat, and on his head was a scarf patterned in red and white and held in place by a black cord. His Cadillac was new and shiny, the interior smooth and leather, the dashboard a sleek walnut. The overall effect for me at seventeen was of wealth and foreignness. Not only was the individual driving the car—the one inviting me to come in, wanting to talk with me—male, and thus automatically alien to someone like me (a girl's girl, soon to become a woman's woman, taught by a protective mother to be distrustful of men, especially strange ones), he was also of a strange culture and caste in the United States, where I lived at that time a middle-class life in a white Christian suburb.

So powerful was my indoctrination by a society that stressed pliability in girls, it was as if I was physically overpowered by a force, an alien force, that took over my body and compelled me to say and do things I didn't want to, things I knew were contrary to my best interests, to my safety. Like a puppet under a puppeteer's control, my mind said one thing and my body did the opposite. I couldn't break the social rules of polite behavior; I couldn't be rude; I couldn't risk offending this person who sat in the car before me, who was himself breaking social rules by cutting someone off as she walked, by asking a girl unknown to him to risk her own safety by getting into a car with a strange man.

What did he want, this strange man? Today—a woman with knowledge and experience, a mother of two sons, an aunt of two nephews and three nieces—I have visions of boys and girls being grabbed off streets and dragged into vans, of men forcing women into cars to be taken away and never heard of again. I know of rape and murder, labor- and sex-trafficking. I know the statistics, always appalling, of women and children exploited or hurt or dead. Yet, looking back, would that kind of predator hunt in a flashy car, wearing what amounted then, in that city and on that street, to a costume?

What he wanted was to recruit me. As an actress. For films. He talked of the star I could become. Even in my immature, still-teenage imagination, I questioned the type of movies this stranger might be talking about. I also questioned the idea of my being beautiful—not realizing then the automatic desirability of the young. But I also didn't have the experience or knowledge to envision, in any clear way, pornography—the vast empire of trafficked women for the pleasure of men.

I survived my experience half-in and half-out of a strange man's car. I was not grabbed and threatened; I was not locked in and driven away. There was much embarrassed demurring and awkward insistence on my part that I needed to discuss with my parents the idea of my acting in films before he gave me his card and asked for my phone number to talk to them himself.

This not only seemed a legitimate move on his part but also freed me, finally, from the conversation, from the man's plans for me, and, most importantly, from the car. I exited through the still-open door and continued walking, with relief, down the street in search of food. I couldn't wait to tell Enika about the encounter, which suddenly seemed more like a cool adventure than a near escape now that I was free.

In the end I did tell my mother about the man, in a more benign way, without including the invitation to enter his car, or my acceptance of this invitation. When the man called she was prepared and told him that her daughter could not act in any films, and that there would be no more contact between us. And that was that.

Yet for years the encounter was for me both gratifying (a man had, after all, "chosen" me as desirable) and mortifying. I recalled all too readily the fidgety sense of powerlessness, the urge to escape, and the barrier to that escape that was my perverse loyalty to a sense of etiquette. It was another manifestation of that familiar in-between space, that limbo, where safety and politeness battled and politeness usually won. It was only good fortune—luck, really—that saved me in those kinds of situations from harm. Now, so much later, I remember that moment in my life with no gratification, less mortification, and more anger. I'm angry that I was socialized by a warped mentality of self-sacrifice over self-preservation that I know is specific to women.

Although I don't have daughters, I want the opposite for the young women of this world: I want righteous confidence for my nieces, for my younger friends, for the next generations.

Not Black or White,
But Gray

(California, 1985)

*I*t's dark when my eyes open. A weight presses on my back, a hardness moves inside me. I struggle, in the darkness of an unfamiliar room in an unfamiliar house, to lift myself from the mattress and dislodge the man whose body traps my own. But I can't. My arms have always been my weakness; I can barely do a regular push-up, let alone one with an added 180 pounds saddled on top of me.

It's strange to remember this now, but at that moment I don't speak or call out; I simply struggle in silence. He, the man who pins me down with his heft and weight, is also quiet. He does not speak, not even when he's finished and rolls off to fall immediately asleep on his side of the bed.

Left alone in solitary wakefulness, I feel a rush of fury. A flash of light, one that seems my anger and outrage embodied, pierces the darkness before I lose consciousness to sleep once again.

I'd never had proper sex with Brian before. He was older, British, reckless to the point of lawlessness, and, to me, exotic. At twenty-five, he seemed suave and savvy; his Cockney accent only added to his appeal. He and his friend, nicknamed "Animal," were traveling the world, visiting San Francisco, having fun. Looking back, I see Animal as Brian's doppel-ganger, his shadow, his alter ego—a sidekick, yes, but also a foil. Physically, he was bigger than Brian, fleshier, and shaggy-haired, as if the artist creating him had used cruder strokes, thicker paint, neglecting to soften rough edges or adjust irregular lines. His speech was coarser, his accent so broad it was almost unintelligible.

Brian picked up on my schoolgirl admiration of his exploits, for he often entertained me with stories of his adventures. Once, the pride obvious in his voice, Brian told me that the weekend before he and Animal had stopped for gas during the early hours of the morning in the city's theater district. When they discovered the station attendant asleep in his kiosk, they'd stealthily filled their tank (this was back when you paid after putting in the gas, and in cash), then one of them steered while the other pushed the car out of the station in neutral, careful not to alert the dozing attendant with the rumble of the engine.

That was the kind of thing they did, never minding that it was illegal or considering that it could jeopardize someone's job. All that was important to them, these "young lads," was the money it saved them. Their attitude, completely foreign to me, titillated; their adventures translated into a strange kind of freedom that I, as a woman, could never have.

At one point that summer, Brian and Animal found a house-sitting job in Tiburon. Built on the edge of the water, the modern mansion's huge windows took full advantage of the view that swept over the Bay and included San Francisco, Angel Island, and the Golden Gate Bridge. I met Brian there once on a warm, dusky evening, Animal notable only for his absence. We drank from large goblets of expensive pinot noir Brian had found in the wine cellar. The glass coffee table in front of us reflected the reds and golds of the sun setting over the water. On the cutting-edge stereo system we listened to Donna Summer, and "Love to

Love You, Baby" throbbed as we drank, the volume on high.

I felt more aware, more alive, with Brian. My senses were aroused when I was with him, to the point that regular life and daily routines transformed: common sounds pulsed into sensual patterns, mundane sights glowed with intensity, ordinary touch became erotic.

Despite the heightened sensuality, the aphrodisiac of age difference, and the exotic accent, I didn't want to have sex with Brian. Although we were intimate, I had told him—and he'd assured me he understood—that intercourse wasn't an option. I had said at least once if not several times as we fooled around kissing and touching, when his hands went past my hips and his body attempted to lie on mine, that I didn't want to "go all the way." When awake, and therefore able to engage, I stopped his hands with my own, pushed him away mid-move, said aloud again: *No*.

So, even at eighteen, I knew what happened that night was wrong. Thinking about it decades later, I wonder at my lack of sustained anger. I know that I didn't like it, that I was offended at a trust betrayed. So I wonder at my willingness, after that night, to continue to see him, even to have sex with him. Although I wasn't a virgin by then, it felt like something as irreparable as a hymen had been destroyed, and there was no point in going back. Rather than make a stand and refuse to see him, or report him to the police and charge him with rape, I told one close friend about it before allowing the relationship to burn itself out, to fade away with the summer and dissipate into a memory— vaguely distasteful, but ultimately harmless. If life were a fairy tale, I think to myself these many years afterward, would that moment in the dark, alone with the Prince who morphed into a Wolf, be the price I had to pay? For growing up? For being naïve? For partaking, however vicariously, however temporarily, in the thrill and power of the forbidden?

I confess that today I cannot remember his real name—the name of the man who disrespected my words, my boundaries, and my trust to violate my body. And this almost frustrates me more than the forced intercourse so many years ago. For decades, until very recently, I remembered his name clearly. First and last. Brian, the name I use here, is but a guess, an approximation. I firmly believe, despite my fuzzy memory on this point, that his name started with a B. And I also believe, but with somewhat less conviction, that its second letter was R. So it could be that his name *was* Brian, or it could be that it was Bruce or Bryce or Brandon. Some people might argue that it makes sense to forget the details of a violation, as in trauma-induced amnesia or the blocking of painful sensations. Why, then, do I continue to remember the details of the violation when I've forgotten the perpetrator's name?

And always on my mind, an unchanging and unchangeable part of that memory, is my decision to sleep all night in the same bed with him, both of us naked under the same covers, without even the flimsiest silk or cotton as a barrier between us. Regardless of the crime he committed, the sin of betrayal against my trust, I clearly put too much faith—naïvely, stupidly—in a twenty-five-year-old man I barely knew outside of bars, clubs, and borrowed suburban mansions. In a utopia, I suppose, anyone could sleep naked next to anyone else and expect the wishes regarding her body to be respected. But we don't live in a utopia and I knew that, even at eighteen.

In a court of law today, as a defendant of my own silence and my willingness to see him again, to sleep with him again, I would talk about the norms and mores in the eighties that accepted men's misbehavior. About a society that indoctrinated girls and women and influenced the legal system. I would say to both judge and jury, "You have to understand that it was the *culture* back then. I judged myself *and* the man. I blamed myself because men getting away with what they could was normal in those days. Yes, rape was a crime, but people thought of date rape as more of a *misunderstanding*."

In order to be fair I must include the man, the perpetrator, the rapist—my misbehaving date—in this scenario. He must also have his moment to defend himself. I imagine he would say something like, "She told me she didn't want to have sex, that she just wanted to fool around, but then when she spent the *whole night* sleeping *completely naked* next to me, I thought she'd changed her mind." If he had a lawyer, the lawyer might add to his defense by also bringing up, as I had, the culture of the times, when the prevalent ethos implied that even if a woman put up a fight against a sexual act being forced on her by her date, even if she resisted physically if not verbally, this was just part of the ritual, the "no means yes" idea that dominated the fifties and sixties and seemingly continued forward into the eighties and beyond. The lawyer could claim that his client was "getting mixed signals."

A lawyer might have to speak for Brian because he was a young man of his times—times when some people like him, white and Christian as well as young and male, felt that they could do what they wanted without guilt or remorse, as long as, of course, they didn't get caught. Oh, to live like that! To have such a persona—one tacitly, implicitly entitled to certain free-doms, even to the illegal or immoral or unethical. No thought. No guilt. No remorse. Although I would never act on such enti-tlement even if I had it, what unimaginable freedom to live unimprisoned—no, *unaware*—of the bars that have caged me all my life, bars that are rules and norms and laws, both spoken and unspoken, both codified and not, reserved for girls and women, for people like me.

What he, the man I saw for a few months in 1985, should have said that night so long ago is, "Hey, I don't think it's a good idea for you to stay the night. I mean, you can, but if you do I'll sleep in another room. It won't work, me lying right next to you all night." In other words, if I had my day in court, I would tell him that he should have been straight with himself and with me, that he should have known the limits to his willpower and warned me. I know this now, that he should have, but I was too young or immature or naïve to know it then.

Thus the fact that I can't remember this man's name bothers me. How can I defend myself in a court of law, or assign blame, even if only hypothetically, even if only in my own imagination, if I can't remember such a central fact as the name of my antagonist? It denotes a lack of control, if not over what actually happened then at least over what I remember and what I don't, and therefore over my own mind, which I always equate with my very selfhood. There's a loss of control when what I want to remember, what I believe I should remember, is gone. It leaves me feeling, even at this point (perhaps especially at this point), a degree of powerlessness: what such an event—an attack in the night, when fast asleep with no defenses—makes one feel.

I still remember that the next morning we pretended nothing untoward had happened. I got up with the sun to escape the room and what had occurred there a few hours before. I was subdued but civil with Brian as he mumbled, only half awake, something about orange juice or coffee from the warm tumbled sheets. At home, where my parents and siblings had yet to rise so early on a Sunday morning, I climbed into bed, the narrow wooden bed my mother slept in when she was a girl in Peru (the same bed that traveled over the decades from Lima to California then to Quito and back) to sleep once again, this time feeling safe in my familiar room and in my familiar house, secure with the stable constant in my life that was my family: mother, father, sister, brother, even dog.

I never did bring up that night to Brian. But what has

haunted me for years is that his friend was nearby on his own mattress. He had entered the shared bedroom after Brian and I fell asleep the first time. What I still remember, and what I still find hard to bear—more traumatizing, perhaps, than the quiet, middle-of-the-night assault, or than the recent forgetting of names, first and last—is the thought that this man, from his own bed on the other side of the room, was watching.

Leaving Henry Higgins

(*California, 1989*)

I 've noticed that a house can reflect the personalities of its owners. My friend Kay's was in a shady neighborhood, overshadowed by clusters of tall redwood trees. Even on the hottest days, this area was dim and cool. Kay's house, itself made of dark wood, was located in a dusky nook of a quiet street. The house was like Kay and her husband, or they were like the house: refined neo-hippie, Northern California Bohemian, a combination of Stevie Nicks and Cat Stevens with a touch of the Gypsy Kings. Inside, its vaguely hippie aesthetic mixed with Spanish scarves, silk drapes, Japanese floor cushions, and Persian carpets, the color palette rich with golds and greens and reds. A baby grand piano, its soft walnut top draped with a fringed throw, held the place of honor in the living room, a spacious area that served as the heart of the home.

One night, at Kay's college graduation party, I wandered around, a glass of merlot in hand. After Kay greeted me at the door, welcoming me with a kiss on the cheek, I mingled with different guests, none of whom I remember today. There was a group outside on the wooden deck, under a vine-covered loggia; there were people in the living room on the low couches, among the thick votive candles placed strategically here and there; another group of guests hovered by the side table in the kitchen that served as a bar. After some time, I searched for a bathroom, tipsy after two full glasses of wine on an empty stomach, and found myself in the master bedroom shared by Kay and her husband. Their large mattress lay on the floor, buried under silky duvets and knitted afghans.

On my way out, I spotted a small painting on top of the dresser and picked it up. It was a watercolor of a couple in a symbolically natural setting: a single tree, a lone star, a full moon. Caught in the moment of erotic embrace, the man faced the viewer, his features obscured by the woman who kissed him, one pale leg up and around him in wanton caress. It was the woman's figure that caught my attention. The flame-red hair, long and loose and wavy, the white skin, delicate and soft, the naked limbs, sylphlike—it was Kay.

There was a riotous sensuality about the nude couple, the amorous pose, which made it seem a profound violation of privacy to even look at it. Yet there it was, propped up and displayed for all who wandered in to see.

I remained standing for a moment in my friend's bedroom, staring at the image in my hands. Eventually, I sank down onto the edge of the bed, still holding the painting. The effect on me of this little painting on paper that was starting to warp, its edges already becoming brittle, was of something intensely private yet at the same time flaunted. It seemed like it was meant to be seen, meant to be viewed—the older, experienced man and the young, beautiful girl; they had everything, and potent sex too. The painting added to my idealization of my friend's marriage, and now I saw the passion as well as the equality, the intimacy and the conscious egalitarianism.

I met Kay in Berkeley, during a college course on gender and psychology. In her earnest feminism, Kay was a kindred spirit. Once she asked me to help demonstrate the gendered body language she was covering as part of a presentation for our class of over two hundred. Using me to roleplay in the large lecture hall, Kay went over the ways that boys and men take up space: legs spread wide and standing firmly upon the ground, they lay claim to their surroundings with their stance; they sit with knees open, crotches flaunted, arms over the backs of chairs and sofas; their handshakes are firm, their gaze direct. Girls and women, trained to draw into themselves and take up the least space possible, sit with legs crossed, arms tucked in, crotches hidden and protected; they tilt their heads, nodding throughout conversations in supportive agreement. Together on the stage, Kay and I shook hands and pretended to converse, taking on the physical roles of male and female.

As we became closer, Kay and I would sometimes discuss her relationship with her husband, an older yet enlightened therapist. I remember eating one hot summer day with them both on the outdoor patio of a restaurant. They sat close to each other under the canvas umbrella, clasped hands resting on the tabletop. I observed them as they ordered from the menu, sipped ice water, ate their focaccia and salads. I noticed how they were careful, compulsively so, to listen to each other, to give each other undivided attention. If her husband accidentally cut Kay off in conversation, he stopped, apologized for his interruption, then turned toward her to listen with a silent intensity. Kay did the same for him. As my boyfriend and I were definitely not that respectful of each other in our own interactions, this behavior between Kay and her husband impressed me as ideal.

*T*wo years after the graduation party and my discovery of the intimate portrait, I drove Kay home after a movie. It was twilight when I maneuvered my Volkswagen through the darkening streets under the redwoods, and perhaps it was this in-between time, dusky and indefinite, that prompted me to talk about nostalgia. How, although still in my early twenties, I felt nostalgic for a more youthful self. How now I felt accustomed to, almost jaded against, the freedom of going out at night. The freedom to cross the Golden Gate Bridge in the cool evening air, with the lights of the city glimmering against the blue-black sky. To feel exhilarated, alive, just by being in the city after nightfall. To click heavy silver lighters and smoke Marlboros. To sit in parked cars drinking cheap wine from Styrofoam cups with friends before entering nightclubs. To trade dinner for cigarettes and alcohol, TV for cafés and dancing. I saw marriage as a closing of doors—a narrowing of options and a blinkering of potential. I'd been with my boyfriend for over six years; it felt as if I had already made a final decision, chosen a single path.

Kay listened in silence. Then, her voice low and thoughtful, she said, "You know what? I haven't had that. I haven't had any of those experiences you're talking about. I left home at fifteen, so I had to work *and* go to school . . . then I got married so young." Kay was realizing, out loud, how she had missed much of that intervening stage, the transitional time in between childhood and adulthood that is about discovery and wonder and awe.

Almost a year later, after I married the man I'd been with for seven years and moved to Seattle, Kay called me. She was divorcing her husband. As part of a post-graduate internship, she had gone abroad for two weeks. During her time away, she'd started to ruminate about her marriage, her life, and our nostalgia conversation.

"Do you remember that night," she asked me, "when we talked about youth and what you miss about being a teenager?"

I did remember. Well, Kay told me, when she arrived back at the airport and saw her husband waiting for her, flowers in hand—her heart sank. She knew right then that she would leave him.

She and her husband started the process of mediation, hoping to avoid costly divorce lawyers. Although the term "mediation" seemed to promise more understanding and less acrimony, there was instead finger-pointing and accusations. At one point, as Kay defended her need for independence, her husband turned on her. "But I *made* you! You are what you are because of *me*!"

She quickly countered, "Who do you think you are, *Henry Higgins*?"

Although Kay and I laughed about that, we also recognized the serious subtext. She had divulged by then that her husband abused her more than once. When I first listened to Kay recount the violence, I imagined her in the living room, shoved backward, falling over the ottoman. Or by the piano, where, in the midst of a shouting match, the husband's hand swings forward to slap his wife's face, making her cheek redden and her eyes water as she stares back at him in disbelief.

"Oh my god . . . Kay . . . I'm so sorry," I had said when she first told me. Shocked, I thought back to the eye-gazing, the intent listening, the clasped hands, the erotic painting in the bedroom. How could the man in that relationship, supposedly enlightened, a self-proclaimed feminist, strike his wife?

The truth of the marriage, Kay confessed, was that it was a façade. The constant hand-holding, the apologies for interruptions, the long, loving looks—those were for public consumption. At home, alone and with no audience, he could become angry and controlling. In the best light, he was acting as a professorial Henry Higgins and thought of himself as a benevolent Pygmalion.

I have one image in my head from before we lost contact. It is Kay's first Halloween as a single woman. She and a group of friends celebrate on Castro Street. Kay is dressed as a female pirate, a prototype of Johnny Depp's kohl-eyed Jack Sparrow: beaded headband, harem pants, fringed sash. As the most celebrated holiday of the year in the Castro district, all the flamboyance, the creativity, the lust for life, is on full display. Kay, in the middle of her group, in the midst of the Mardi Gras–like revelers taking up the whole, crowded, lit-up street, dances with abandon.

One day, curious, I decide to try and find out what happened to my friend in the last two decades. Did Kay fulfill her dream of getting a PhD? Of having a successful career? Of becoming self-sufficient? When I look her up, I discover that she works for a large corporation. Multiple degrees and titles follow her name in an impressive row. But what stands out to me the most is Kay's hair. The online photograph shows it straight, trimmed, tamed. It's still red, but it's no longer the wild, beautiful, pre-Raphaelite mane that once framed her thin, elegant face.

I expand the picture on the screen and study it for clues, much like I did once with the watercolor I found in Kay's bedroom. I wonder about the woman who once fought to be free, to create nostalgic memories, to throw off the suffocating paternalism that masqueraded as devoted attachment, and hope that somewhere—despite time and age, underneath the academic degrees and corporate titles—she's still there.

On Silence and Voice

(*California, 1986*)

*I*n college, a Gender Studies professor taught us how patriarchy demands silence from women. An ideal femininity is
a quiet one, soft and demure, with no hard edges or strident
noises. Now, over thirty years later, it seems that as a culture
we are—at least beginning to be—more open, more introspective
about our problem with labeling women and men differently.
About how we think of women who speak out as aggressive,
ugly in their obvious power plays, while men who do so are
considered assertive, strong and worthy of respect. But in that
classroom during the mid-eighties, this information felt new to
me, and, more than that, it felt exciting, powerful, radical. If we
believe that our identities as women, as inferior and weak and
defenseless, are constructed, then we can find ways to counter
these constructions. We can learn to speak, to use language to
create ourselves, to use words as bricks to build solid, lasting
definitions of women as complex and whole human beings.

Those many years ago in that classroom, did I associate the
labels my father and mother had given me growing up—that
they continued to give me—with the cultural tropes that circum-
scribe girls and women? I don't recall. But now, in my middle
age, as a mother, I see the connection. Whenever I protested
too much or too loudly, my father silenced me by saying, *Don't
be strident.* My mother, when she thought I was being too bossy

or directive or opinionated, often said, *Pareces un sargento*. *Strident* and *sargeant* — words that shame a girl who is trying to become her best self among competing and conflicting pressures: be intelligent, be feminine, be confident, be soft spoken, be knowledgeable, be deferential, be ladylike, be strong, modest, sexy, smart, pretty, quiet, sweet . . .

One example amid all the theory caught my attention. Many women internalize the ideal of feminine silence so that they cannot call for help, *even in extreme danger*. The professor described self-defense classes that suggested women go into closed cars and *practice screaming*. It sounded ridiculous, yet I did wonder, as I sat among the tiered rows of desks taking assiduous notes in my binder, if I could scream on demand, loudly and unapologetically, to save myself.

I took what I saw as a challenge — it might have been an actual assignment — and a few days later tried the exercise. I went alone to the family car, a big silver sedan, and made sure the doors and windows were tightly closed and there was no one in sight. Assured that I was fully cocooned within, I took a deep breath, opened my mouth, and . . . tried to scream.

A scream is different from a shout or a howl or even a shriek. It requires sustained volume and intensity. That day in the car, it took me several attempts to achieve. Part of the problem was lack of practice, but part of it was, distressingly, embarrassment. I was embarrassed in front of myself, for myself. I didn't need an audience; I was already judgmental enough. Although my mind was saying otherwise, my instincts — the social ones that had replaced the natural ones we're all born with — held me back. Mocked me. Made me hesitant and uneasy.

A few months later, in that same driveway where I'd practiced screaming in a closed car, the small motorcycle I drove then skidded on the wet leaves that had accumulated during an autumnal shower, throwing me to one side as it crashed with a roar on the other. I managed to stand, but after a few steps in the direction of our neighbors' house (a house much nearer to me than my own) my body seized and refused to move any further. Although I felt no pain at that point, I was held back from greater damage by my physical instincts: looking down, I saw my knee swollen to the size of a grapefruit, straining against the denim of my jeans.

That's when I spied Mrs. Sheldon moving in front of her living room window. I raised my voice in an attempt to get her attention. I needed help. I couldn't very well balance precariously on my one good leg at the end of my driveway forever. But I wasn't able to. I only managed a small call for help, more like a squawk, that no one heard. I tried again, and again I couldn't yell loudly enough to attract anyone's notice—not Mrs. Sheldon's, not any neighbor who might have been in their yard, not that of a driver in a passing car. I began to despair; it seemed I was muzzled as well as paralyzed, made mute by an internalization of what it meant to be feminine, attractive, worthy.

Minutes later, Mrs. Sheldon appeared at the wheel of her car, preparing to exit our shared driveway. When she reached the fallen motorcycle, she opened her door and stepped out to ask if I was okay. I burst into tears.

Ten Dollars

(Los Angeles, 1991)

he clock strikes midnight. I was feeling safe up to
this point, but now, in these first seconds of the
brand-new day, with the night still young for the partying set,
the music stops, the disco lights slow, a spotlight beams onto
the stage, and a voice—disembodied, male—announces the start
of an event. Most women, perhaps smarter than me, slip away
into the shadowy corners, to the more neutral territory of the
bar, to the safety of the bathroom. Most men—safe, complacent,
eager for the coming attraction—stay.

Although I know there are all kinds of men in the dance
hall—tall, short, drunk, stoned, hairy, clean shaven, muscular,
lean—they all seem the same to me. Their fists pump, almost en
masse, as a young woman parades across the stage. I watch them
as they watch the young woman, who wears what seems to be
the requisite uniform: tiny triangles of Lycra on her breasts and
floss-thin strings between buttock cheeks. She gyrates to the
music on platform heels, her aim maximum sensuality, because
she knows the dancer with the most enthusiastic reaction wins
five hundred dollars. The almost exclusively male audience
obliges, whooping and whistling, their shouts melding in mob
excitement, when this first "girl" exits the stage and another
replaces her.

The more provocative the dancer's moves, the louder the

cheers. In the increasing frenzy, these cheers take on a different quality, with undercurrents of something like contempt, and start to sound more like jeers. But then—abruptly—it's over. The stage darkens, giant speakers again pound out rhythmic bass, people resume dancing as if nothing has happened.

But I cannot.

*E*arlier that summer night in 1991, my friend and I found advertised in the local paper a nightclub that featured our favorite kind of music. In our early twenties, young and relatively poor, we were determined to have a fun night out, but it had to be on a budget. I remember analyzing the small blurb before committing to a plan. I made sure of the location (near Beverly Hills), the music (a mixture of pop and rap), the hours (nine to two), the price of admission (ten dollars), and, most crucially, the absence of two words: *bikini contest*.

We ate dinner beforehand at a restaurant where we stretched the little money we had by sharing a chopped salad and multiple baskets of free bread, our usual strategy for dining at more expensive venues. Then I drove us in my car, a sturdy Volkswagen Jetta, to the club. To park, we had to leave the city streets and pass through spiked iron gates into a walled complex—which, in retrospect, evoked the atmosphere of a fortress or a compound. Once inside the hall, we joined the throng of revelers dancing to the DJ's trendy medleys, drinks from the bar in hand.

*T*hat night at the club, the contestants sell themselves for the chance of winning cash. Their faces shimmer with perspiration, lips fixed in a smile as they move, each in turn, alone in the hot circle of light. I watch as the men cheer and whistle; they are greedy, grasping for what they assume belongs to them. An anger surges within me that is intense yet also, undercut as it is by a familiar sense of powerlessness, desperate.

I feel alone, as if I'm the only person in the club, in the city, in the country, who cares. Does anyone else think the way I do? Looking at the young women dancing on the stage, I don't see sensuality, I don't see beauty, I don't see any kind of joy or creativity; instead I see vulnerability—bodies exposed for consumption, shiny cars at a dealership, animals in a zoo.

When it finally ends it's as if I've just awoken from a bad dream, but rather than a welcome sense of relief there's instead the claustrophobia of a continuing nightmare. I realize I've been standing rigid with tension, arms crossed in front of me, in the middle of the dance floor for the entire contest—a lone woman surrounded by a sea of men. Like them I've been riveted by a spectacle, but not that of the near-naked women. I've been obsessed by the spectacle of these same men objectifying the dancers, of their gaze, the male gaze, converting humans who happen to be female, people who are also women, into commodities. Moments like these make me imagine the documentaries that might be produced in the future about our culture, a culture that defines fully half of the human population—the female half—as objects, sexual or otherwise, to use and abuse and exploit. What kind of talking head would be featured in such a film—a professor, a researcher, a human rights activist, a retired sex worker, a trafficking survivor? Regardless of any future documentary, I find I can't let go and pretend that a bikini contest, with all its blatant commodification of human beings, is normal.

Turning, I squeeze my way through the crowd of men and head toward the bar, where I ask to speak to the manager. The bartender shrugs his shoulders. He'll "see what he can do." The mild confusion with which he considers my request makes me question my decision; my resolve wavers, and what shone brightly a moment ago, clear and defined, flickers, unstable, a fading hologram. Yet I refuse to give up, and I wait by the bar, tense with adrenaline.

A few minutes later, a stocky man with a brush of blond hair approaches, scowling with irritation. Hurrying to me, he leans in until his face is inches from mine. "What do you want?"

Self-conscious, I rush my words: "I need a refund—I'm against bikini contests and don't want to support them—you didn't advertise the contest—that's false advertising—so I want my ten dollars back."

His brow contracts in disbelief. "You got a problem with us?" He grabs my shoulders and shakes me. "Are you *drunk*? Why don't you just get out of here? YOU'RE A BITCH! A CRAZY BITCH!"

Crazy bitch? *Crazy bitch?*

I'm suddenly hyper-aware of gripping hands, digging fingers, spitting lips. Any buzz from the cheap wine I drank previously is gone, and the softened edges from the alcohol sharpen like glass shards against this new threat—what was before merely ideological has become, quite quickly, not only personal but physical. I slip into an out-of-body sensation where part of me watches the action as if offstage, from the sidelines. I feel like I'm in a surreal movie where strange, bad things are happening that shouldn't. Without thinking, I speak again.

"Get. Your. Hands. *Off Me.*"

The manager snatches his hands back, then just as abruptly disappears into the masses milling around the bathrooms and moving toward the exit. The evening has ended. More and more people stream out the door toward the parking lot, slipping on spilled drinks and stumbling over empty bottles, dirty napkins, and broken straws on the sticky floor. I can't see my friend anywhere, and I forget about my ten dollars. I need to find my friend.

Then, out of the corner of my eye, I glimpse her among the club patrons leaving through the hall's double doors. Still tipsy, she shouts something at a dancer, who shouts something back. In a glance I notice the young woman's big bleached hair, cropped top and lacy short shorts, white patent leather stilettos. The next moment the fight escalates and they start shoving each other.

Again, the feeling that I'm the unwilling actor in a surreal movie with an absurd plot—how can this be happening?

But things only get worse. When I start to run toward my friend, out of nowhere security men in orange uniforms surround me. One of them orders, "You have to leave *now*."

At this point we're in the enclosed parking lot from which everyone is departing. Hearing the young woman shriek about contestants like herself needing money—*how dare you judge us!*—I realize my friend has taken up my cause. My heart thuds, my chest feels tight. With great effort I tamp down surging adrenaline. I say out loud what I know to be true—*I'm not leaving without my friend*. Instead of obeying the guards by heading toward my Volkswagen, I deliberately walk in the opposite direction as they tail me. Everywhere car doors slam, engines start, and people call out to one another until, in what seems like seconds, almost everyone's gone. It's quiet in the dark, walled complex. Without the crowds, I can see my friend across the lot, and what I see again doesn't seem real. She's being shuffled off by a second phalanx of security guards, her wrists shackled behind her in handcuffs, her face searching desperately over a shoulder for me. Absurdity has slipped into horror.

Forcing myself to concentrate, I walk slowly toward the Jetta. The guards don't know which of the few cars still scattered in the lot is mine, so I'm able to take a circuitous route, giving myself time to think as I repeat my mantra: "I'm not leaving without my friend . . . I'm not leaving without my friend . . ."

A few feet from the Volkswagen, I spy my compact Canon lying on the backseat. That's when I get an idea. Taking the keys from my pocket, in a matter of seconds I've dashed to the car, unlocked the door, and grabbed the camera—which will become, as soon as I turn around, a kind of James Bond secret-agent weapon.

Swiveling back to face the men, I start snapping pictures.

The effect is instantaneous. It's as if I hold a gun or a grenade. At a time before cell phones and easy recordings, a camera as witness is unexpected. The guards turn and run, shouting to each other, "She's got a camera! She's taking pictures!" In an almost comic reversal of roles, all of a sudden I'm the chaser, the predator, the intimidator, while they, like frightened deer or stampeding sheep, run away yelling for their mates to release the prisoner. Once more, if this is a film, a surreal film, it's dipping into the absurd. Whatever it is, however, I'm part of it, caught in it, and I have to play my part. I chase the fleeing guards with the camera, still taking pictures, while they lead me to my friend. As they charge at her, she panics.

I still remember looking at the photograph, developed the next day at a nearby drugstore. My friend, mascara smudged and lipstick smeared like an actress in a B-movie poster, cries with fear and confusion as she backs away from the approaching guards.

As soon as she's released, my friend rushes toward me. I whisper the plan: walk quickly, but *don't run*. I worry that running might trigger a pack animal mentality; I know hikers are warned not to run from mountain lions, and my instincts tell me the same principle applies to the pack of guards watching us leave: two vulnerable females, unarmed except for a camera, our backs exposed and unprotected.

When we finally arrive at the car, we jump in. "Lock your door! Lock your door!" I almost yell as I put the engine into gear and speed out of the complex, half expecting the heavy gates to close on us before we can escape. For it feels like an escape. It *is* an escape. Again—we're in a movie, this time some kind of woman-in-jeopardy action film. My friend tells me, once she's calmed down enough to debrief, that she overheard a male clubber asking one of the guards why they had her in handcuffs.

We're saving her for later.

Although my arms and legs tremble with residual adrenaline, I'm excited by the evidence of illegality, of wrongdoing, that my photographs will provide. I think I can gain control of the plot at this point, and determine the end. I talk about returning the next day to the club armed with this proof and again demanding a refund.

But my friend has other ideas. She wants all of it to go away. In this metaphor of scripts and films, she's the protagonist and now also the director in a drama where she can manipulate the ending to her satisfaction rather than mine. She fears the hurt her father will feel if he sees the pictures. I know her father well and can imagine the mild, sweet-mannered man, who loves a cup of Earl Grey in the mornings and *Masterpiece Theatre* after dinner, looking at the photographs, his confused frown deepening into horror as he takes in the images of his daughter in handcuffs, terrorized by strange men. He is an emotional man—or, to be more precise, he is a man who shows his emotions. And I'm certain that, looking at these pictures of his beloved only child, he would cry.

Thinking of this father, I too become protective of him, even as my mind turns to my own father with his serious expression and black-rimmed glasses. My father doesn't cry. He rarely shows his emotions. But I know a photo of me, vulnerable and threatened, would disturb him to his core. How could he make sense of a daughter violated despite her upbringing, her education, her loving family?

What my friend is telling me is that she wants to shield her father from pain. That she needs to sacrifice justice for him. That because this is *her* father, her violation and her reputation, she's the one who should decide how to edit the script.

Later, she will destroy the photographs.

Looking back to that night three decades ago, I see that I was naïve not once, but twice. I was naïve when I believed that in standing up for my principles by using my voice, a voice that on the surface at least was determined and unwavering, I would succeed in my efforts. I spoke up, although it was embarrassing, even humiliating—I was too unimportant to the bartender, even in my strange behavior, to warrant investment in my quest. I spoke up to the manager, then found a way to extricate myself from his manhandling of my person. Yet I was unprepared for the possibility of a gang of security guards handcuffing a young woman because she was weaker than them, with the plan to rape her when everyone had left the premises and they could act without witness. The second time I was naïve was with my friend's refusal to seek retribution, even in the form of ten dollars. Her desired ending to the night's unexpected narrative of innocence and naïvetee, of brutal objectification and dangerous chauvinism, was one that spared a beloved father pain. At that moment I had to hold two truths in my mind, as equals, and acknowledge that sometimes there isn't one single, perfect solution.

That night so many years ago, I drove my car, familiar and dependable, away from the club that had become dark and nightmarish, a cursed place as surreal as a Salvador Dalí landscape, as dangerous as an exploitation film, to the safety of my friend's apartment. While we waited at a stoplight, an SUV full of partying college boys pulled up next to us near the tony UCLA campus. When they passed, amid drunken sounds of laughter and jeering, one boy hefted his backside off the passenger seat and up to the window, pulled down his jeans, and mooned us, fleshy white buttocks flattened against the glass.

Harry Denton's

(San Francisco, 1991)

I was glad of what I was wearing that night at Harry Denton's, because this club wasn't the kind I usually frequented. I was in my early twenties, finished with college, taking a couple of years off before graduate school. A group of us had gathered beforehand at the house where one of the girls worked as a full-time nanny. Her employer was recently divorced, with two young children. We were all loosely friends—my sister and I and this handful of girls with whom we'd grown up, all daughters of Peruvian mothers who had married Anglo men, either American or English or Irish. They had bonded in San Francisco when still single women, drawn together by their Peruvian roots, by their knowledge of Limenean ways and customs, by having attended the same Catholic high school, an all-girl institution guarded by nuns wearing black and white habits rather than coats of mail.

If these mothers could have seen where we were going that night, to this particular nightclub with its polished brass and waxed mahogany, with its well-stocked bar and wealthy clientele, they would have been happy, or at least they would have approved. They'd had similar dreams for themselves, when young and newly immigrated, to those they had now for their daughters: marry before thirty and marry well, start a family, continue the assimilation they'd begun in their own lives with their migrations and their marriages.

I remember this divorced father's townhouse on the Marina in the city, across the Golden Gate Bridge from my own home in the northern suburbs. This house, in a traditionally expensive neighborhood of San Francisco, was sparsely decorated to my eye, which was habituated to the patterns and textures of Persian carpets and Peruvian oil paintings, to the rich brown of a leather coffee table and the warm mahogany of a piano, to shelves stocked with my parents' books—Japanese, engineering, philosophy, and *Tom Brown's School Days* on my father's side; and on my mother's, Mario Vargas Llosa as well as Spanish translations of *War and Peace*, *Madame Bovary*, and *Pride and Prejudice*. In contrast, this place was white—white walls and cabinets and decorative shelves, the carpet a cool ivory, the coffee table a clear glass. It looked decorated by a professional, someone called in to take care of what I assume the ex-wife once had in this divorced man's previous place, the one he had shared with his young family when it was still intact.

As we prepared to leave the well-appointed house, our friend the nanny announced that her employer, the divorced father, was coming with us to the club. This was eyebrow-raising news to me. We were a group of young women—at twenty-four, I was the oldest—and this man must have been at least thirty-five, probably nearing forty. It felt strange, creepy, that he would come with us on a night free of his children to a club, that he would *want* to come with us, that he failed to find such a plan inappropriate. This divorced father and ex-husband clearly belonged to a generation older than the rest of us, in years, certainly, but most importantly in stage of life. Yet here he was—white, clean-shaven, brown-haired, of medium height and medium build, looking like an extra on a film like *Wall Street*—ready to join a group of young women, some still in college, on a Saturday outing to a nightclub.

Harry Denton's could best be described with words such as

swanky, expensive, luxurious, and yuppie; it was both established and had become Establishment. The bouncer was a man
who acted as if he were an official guard, a protective outside
butler, a porter with power. This place was not like the underground clubs I'd frequented, with excitement bordering on awe,
when I was sixteen, seventeen, eighteen years old. Those clubs
hadn't even had bouncers, and could best be described with
such words as temporary and unlicensed and illegal, or plywood,
sheetrock, and naked light bulbs. Unlike the authoritative Harry
Denton's, their names were Noh Club, Minna, Next, and
Nightbreak. My mother would have been appalled if she had
seen those clubs—their dilapidated exteriors hidden deep down
isolated alleys, their unfinished interiors and weird-looking at-
tendees, their music, their fashions, their small counterculture
intimacy.

To those clubs some boys wore makeup and skirts and
chandelier earrings, as did the girls, who also sometimes wore
oversized blazers from thrift stores, army jackets, or tuxedo
shirts tucked into long, thin skirts. The latter combination was
one of my favorites. Another was a black T-shirt whose neck I
cut wide and left unhemmed, and that I wore tucked into a full
skirt my mother had made, to my exact specifications, out of a
red and black plaid crêpe. I cinched this skirt at the waist with
a leather belt I'd bought for a couple of dollars at a thrift store
on Haight Street. A classmate of my younger sister once wanted
to borrow this skirt to go to a school dance, but wasn't allowed
to in the end because it didn't pass muster with her conservative
mother. The problem wasn't the length, pattern, or color, but
instead a stain near the bottom hem where I'd spilled some
black polish while painting my nails. I'd forgotten all about the
stain when I lent the skirt to my sister's friend; it had become
invisible to me among the black and red squares by then. But
when this classmate of my sister returned my skirt, neatly folded

and unworn, I felt a familiar kind of shame spread hotly inside me that meant that I wasn't good enough, that I had failed in some way.

That's when I began to realize that clothes can be weaponized, or at a minimum curated for their protective qualities. They can be a kind of armor to select with care because they represent a certain identity to the world. There's a sense of agency, of power, in choosing one's clothes. You could call it donning a mask or creating a costume; the mundane task of getting dressed transforms into a purposeful creativity that signals a particular persona.

That night at Harry Denton's I had no doubt about my outfit, and I walked through the heavy double doors held open by the bouncer fully confident in its appropriateness. This turned out to be fortuitous, for I would need that freedom from insecurity to navigate the next few hours. The best uniforms do this—the ones warriors, soldiers, and martial artists wear, as well as athletes (think of acrobats, runners, or footballers)—they enhance performance rather than hinder it. That night I wore high heels, sophisticated rather than office-y, and a silk sarong-style skirt over a black bodysuit with a scooped neckline. But the finishing touch, the pièce de résistance, was the jacket. This jacket I had discovered, like a pirate looking for long-buried treasure or an ornithologist for a rare white heron, on the crowded sale racks in the Back Room of Loehmann's. It was by some designer, I can't recall which now, but what counts is that it was "Made in Italy," and that the fit was superb, the cut precise, the shoulders crisp, the waist nipped in just so. The material was soft and supple yet thick enough to hold its shape. To me, accustomed as I was to clothes found in thrift stores or made by my mother, it was a treasure indeed. I could go anywhere—even a ritzy, conservative nightclub full of suit-clad, cognac-drinking finance men, bankers sporting money clips and red faces—with assurance.

What did we do at Harry Denton's that evening? It wasn't my idea of fun, because the atmosphere was too stiff, too—as another, prior, generation might describe it—"square." I'm sure there was the buying of drinks at the bar, the clustering in pairs or threesomes to sip our drinks and observe our surroundings, the dancing with each other or the older employer who accompanied us that night. I always, however, had an eye out for my sister; older in years and, I believed, more experienced, I assumed responsibility for her. I didn't want her to get into any trouble, or come to any kind of harm. I didn't want her misused, discomfited, hurt, harassed, or pressured by some man, some predatory stranger at a nightclub.

Curiously, although I'm confident in my recollection of what I wore that night, I'm not sure what my sister wore. There are no photos to serve as record, to take out and examine for clues as to the hard facts of that night. Somehow, though, in reliving the night so many years later, I see her in a creamy silk dress, one she owned and wore to more formal events, one with matching piping, wide sleeves, and a modest length. It doesn't escape me that this outfit my sister wears in my memory evokes, in both color and style, a kind of purity and innocence.

An hour into our time at Harry Denton's, sex was had in the men's bathroom. Inside one of the stalls. I saw thin, stockinged ankles and high heels under the locked door. Were they positioned so that I could see the bottom of the soles, the tips of the heels? Arranged in such a way that it was clear a woman was on her knees on the sticky tile floor?

I don't recall. Nor do I remember what I was doing trying to use the men's bathroom. Perhaps the women's was broken, or full, and I thought I could run in and do my business quickly, without much fanfare, without being noticed. I do remember, however, stopping my sister from coming in as I was leaving the bathroom. She had discovered where I was and wanted to follow me inside. I didn't want her to see what I saw as sordid, as corrupt and potentially corrupting.

Not too long after I guided my sister away from the bathroom, there was a crash as its door banged open and two brawling men spilled out, stumbling and clutching ineffectually at each other—not at all elegant, not at all choreographed, not at all dignified. Instead there was tripping and pushing and rolling around on the floor. Grunts and pants and shouts.

I stepped back automatically from the men who'd just burst out of the same door we'd recently exited, for I was standing mere feet away from the bathroom's entrance, then pushed my sister behind me in an effort to put myself between her and their drunken, flailing limbs. My mother used to have a similar instinctive gesture when I was growing up. We always drove in sedans with long bench seats in the front where two, three, even four passengers could squeeze in beside the driver. Often I sat right next to my mother as she drove, loving any proximity to her when I was a child. I never wore a seatbelt; in those days seatbelts were considered unnecessary accessories, most of the time ignored until they were forgotten altogether. Whenever my mother was forced to brake suddenly, her right arm automatically shot out in front of my body, protecting me from the possibility of hitting the dashboard.

At Harry Denton's, I watched the men, my sister close behind me, until their fight fizzled out. All their initializing adrenaline was spent within a minute, and the small crowd that had gathered dispersed back onto the dance floor, or the bar, or to sit at one of the small round tables in the lounge.

We left the club shortly afterward. As is often the case after hours of drinking and dancing and posing in a close environment, an environment designed for facile intimacy, things began to unravel, men to rage and women to vomit in toilets, shirts to wrinkle and dampen with sweat, stockings to run and heels to scuff. It felt good to get outside where the night was cool and invigorating. It felt like leaving another world, an underworld of sorts, an overly warm, claustrophobically luxurious cavern. The oppressive feeling of the club's interior came from its overt masculinity, which read to me as a relentless, albeit normalized, machismo: the money and the suits, the alcohol, the sex, and the violence — the entitlement.

Somewhat shell-shocked, my sister and I waited for the rest of our party to gather their sweaters or jackets or handbags from the coat check and emerge from the club doors. When the original group finally came together, I left my sister and our friends behind to walk the divorced father a few yards to his parked car. Approaching the gathering group, the older man had stopped in front of me and, lowering his voice just enough to make his comments confidential, asked, "Can I talk to you?"

After strolling up the block from the club's entrance, we stood under a lamppost, the night mist gathering white under its light, as he retrieved his car keys from a trouser pocket. I don't remember a word we said. Or even if any mild flirtation beforehand (drinks at the bar, maybe a conversation on the dance floor with moving lips close to cocked heads) had led to his request that I walk with him to the parking lot. But what happened next remains very distinctly in my memory. The divorced man, taller than me, tilted his head down and kissed me on the mouth. Although taken by surprise, I didn't draw back in shock; I didn't push him away from me with my palms against his chest; I certainly didn't slap him across the face: *How dare you?*

He finished the kiss and, after bidding me good night, got into his Volvo and drove away. As I watched the car disappear down the street, I tried to figure out how I felt about the night and the club and, of course, the kiss. I'd never kissed a man so much older than me, at least fifteen years older, and I had no intention of kissing him or ever seeing him again in my entire life. Although the kiss had come as a surprise, I didn't feel violated, or taken advantage of. This may have been because in the series of seamy events that night the kiss was the least so; it could have been because I had spent the entire evening in the self-imposed role of the mature one, a kind of leader of the younger girls; it may have been because, acutely conscious of my duty as big sister, I felt like I had control over the situation—with four years more experience than my younger sister, I assumed I could handle such an event better than her; it could have been a combination of these factors.

Thinking about the kiss today, it's somehow tethered to the moment that night when I found myself in the men's bathroom, aware of sex in a stall. I don't remember how I got there; I only know I was standing in my black fitted jacket and silk skirt, among the row of sinks, facing a locked door behind which emanated the sounds of sex that often can be mistaken for duress or pain. I remember that one moment of realization—there was sex happening in the stall—and reaction: I was repulsed, disgusted. There was no sense of titillation or arousal. I felt for the woman—how much pleasure could she be getting out of that moment, in the men's bathroom, her knees on the hard, cold floor, crowded in by metal walls, a toilet bowl, and a man's groin? Would she have chosen this act—at this time, in this place, with this man even—if she were completely free from the expected roles of young women in the complicated choreography that is first attraction and flirtation, then commitment and marriage?

When I try to pinpoint the exact reason for my being in the men's bathroom in the first place, the closest I can get is that I was in that passionate stage of life when hormones and emotions frequently coalesce into an intense pitch. Much of my outrage at the world around me centered on women and the injustices I saw everywhere perpetrated against them, against *us*. It isn't a coincidence that boys sign up on impulse for the military when still teenagers, that the Mormon Church sends out its young members at eighteen to travel the world for two years and proselytize, and that cults know to target youth for recruitment. My husband tells me he reached his peak of religiosity at nineteen, when for a year he went to mosques on Fridays and studied the Quran. I watched his younger brother at dinner parties ten years later, also at nineteen, excuse himself with other devotees to perform ablutions and pray facing east in a separate room.

My own youthful pitch of religiosity focused not on my inherited Catholicism but on the philosophy of human equality that is Feminism. My devotion at that time translated into acts of defiance against the oppressive regime, Patriarchy. I was prone in my early twenties to trying to upend the expectations of me as a young woman, as if striding into a restaurant where paunchy men dine on steak while smoking cigars to overturn a table, sending plates and silverware and the vase full of hothouse roses scattering every which way. My personality then had an aspect of bravado that reminds me now of the poster of Rosie the Riveter: bold, assured, audacious. My boldness, even when a façade, lay not in performing a man's job but in defying women's roles. So I can imagine that at that age I would have grown impatient with a long line at the women's restroom and decided to use the men's, the restroom that never had a line because it always had enough stalls and sinks (not to mention urinals), and which therefore somehow signified a privilege forbidden me as a second-class citizen.

Although it's true that the kiss that night outside of Harry Denton's didn't bother me on a personal level—it certainly didn't traumatize me in any way—what did give me a persistent sense of discomfort was that for the entire duration of the kiss I had the sense at the periphery of my being, even with my eyes closed and my lips engaged, that my sister saw it. I cared more about preserving her innocence, my four-years-younger sister's innocence, than about my own corruptibility. It was a feeling I came to know intimately a decade later, when I had my first child; as a mother, the protective instinct is strong, at times overpowering, and I've embraced it unquestioningly. In my twenties, even as my feminist principles were still maturing, I found myself that night at Harry Denton's, at this club alien to me in its patriarchal presumptions, feeling like the defender and protector of my sister.

In my role as her shield, being kissed by an inappropriately older man, a virtual stranger, held no threat for me. But in my role as filter (again, self-imposed), of straining back the ugly and seamy before it could reach her, what did bother me for a long time afterward was the thought that she'd been exposed to something sordid, even in a small way, and may have been disturbed by it.

The Most Important Quality

(*Peru, 1990*)

*a*t a traditional Peruvian restaurant in Lima, we choose from a menu that offers anticuchos and ceviche, as well as chicha morada, the sweet purple drink made from Incan corn. The décor is darkly Spanish Colonialist, and I sit with my uncle and older cousin on carved chairs with leather seats at a table surrounded by gilt-framed mirrors and gloomy paintings of virgins and saints. Behind me, a large picture window looks onto a small courtyard lush with green. Ferns and palm fronds press against the glass at my back.

Waiting for the food to come, I trace the indented lines in the wood of the table with nails varnished a vivid red. Visiting Peru means feeling dull and plain, like a brown hen, in comparison with the bright peacocky colors and careful makeup of my cousins and aunts. This night I've tried to keep up with a manicure, extra mascara, and even a silky summer dress whose pinks and reds are a huge departure from my customary grays and blacks, the colors I consider chic in the US.

My uncle asks casually, conversationally, "*¿Qué creen que es la cualidad más importante en un esposo?*" He wants to know what quality in a husband we consider the most important.

Although I'm still unmarried, my feminism makes me very invested in this question, and I answer right away with "*¡Inteligencia!*"

"Ahhh," reacts the cousin, her groomed eyebrows raised, as she taps a cigarette expertly on the edge of a brass ashtray. "Not wealth or good looks?"

Like many of my relatives in Peru, Susanna is chic and sophisticated. Unlike most of them, though, she is blonde, and also an only child. And when she was a young girl, apparently, her mother pushed her away, refusing her affection and rejecting her touch. I remember Tía Kitty exclusively in her old age; to me she was mild-mannered and sweet, her skin pale and soft, her face always quietly beautiful. But when her daughter was still a toddler, she was diagnosed with tuberculosis. In trying to protect Susanna from infection, Tía Kitty kept her at arm's length. There was no hugging or kissing or cuddling between mother and child. Instead there was distance from the mother and loneliness for the daughter. Family legend posits that this traumatized Susanna to the point where she now lacks empathy, unable to connect with others in a true and trusting way.

At seventeen, Susanna married—perhaps, I think now, to leave what to her was a cold and unfriendly home. Her husband was a little older than her and magnetically attractive, like the young Richard Gere in *American Gigolo*. But alas there was little difference between her new family and her old. With her husband there was no real bonding. When she was pregnant, he often came home in the early morning darkness "stinking of whore." "Can you imagine?" she would say, as she talked to my mother, "*¡Apestaba a puta!*"

Susanna lasted ten years and three sons before she left the Gigolo for Sebastian, a handsome, painfully elegant bachelor from Britain. He turned out to be too cold and stiff, too rigid. (Years from now, I will learn of a young secretary, a possible affair.) In any case, like Goldilocks, Susanna only found a lasting, viable option with her third try. When she met a sexy Frenchman on the beach during a European vacation one summer, she divorced her soft-spoken Englishman.

She tells us, this night over red wine and pisco sours, that she lets her French husband think he rules the roost; she ensures he believes he is the one who calls the shots and makes the final decisions in their home overlooking the Riviera. Lighting another cigarette, she says that in reality it is she who manipulates behind the scenes to get her own way. She's careful to find the right time to broach a difficult subject, often pampering him with drinks and favorite meals before she does so. She confesses even to lying and dissimulating to get her needs met. But her attitude is not one of a penitent before her priest. She is proud of the strategies that allow her to appear soft and yielding while still getting what she wants. These strategies remind me of a child fooling a parent—a girl, for example, who kisses her mother good night in flannel pajamas only to sneak out her bedroom window after changing in the dark to join friends at a party.

I bristle at this self-satisfied story, offended on behalf of all women by my cousin's complacent claims to a kind of power I find servile. Yet this type of indignation is not new to me. I'm growing accustomed to feeling defensive, especially with my mother's family. Their culture is different from ours in the US, to be sure, yet there's something in that difference that speaks to time, especially generational time. I converse, this night at the traditional Peruvian restaurant, with two relatives older than me, a full generation older, and our age differences seem to blend with our cultural differences to make me feel almost as if we're speaking separate languages.

I am righteous in my feminism. At this time, still in university, unmarried, living in my parents' house, I view the world and its people through binaries. There is them and there is us. There is feminism and there is patriarchy. There is noble resistance and evil oppression. Thinking in binaries blinkers me—I can't see anything in between extremes. I want to prove to my uncle and my cousin that they are wrong and I am right. Girding myself for battle, I think in slogans: *I am a feminist and I will fight!* They must see—I will force them to see.

Even as I argue my points, arrows slung one after the other, trying to hit a target—*What about women, aren't they just as competent as men? . . . Why should the husband always be the boss? . . . Yes, there are differences, but women and men are equal . . . Times have changed, women can get educated, have careers, make money . . . Some men don't want submissive wives and most women want independence and self-sufficiency*—I can tell no one is taking me seriously. My arrows miss their mark and fall to the ground.

They may see what, at this time, I do not: that life is complicated and messy and unfair. That it is unpredictable and cannot be controlled. That faith, in any religion or philosophy or discourse, is not necessarily transformational. Or, on the other hand, they don't. They may be living day by day, relentlessly cheerful, focusing on the present and not interested in philosophical questions. I know I've never heard any of my Peruvian relatives discuss disturbing subjects or problematic ideologies. Nevertheless, tonight my cousin and my uncle probably view me as a woman in her early twenties, barely experienced, one-dimensional in her belief system.

When I recall Susanna's words that night at José Antonio's, the restaurant steeped in the history of Spanish conquest, serving the most traditional of colonial Peruvian food, I imagine her in the living room in Sette, the small village an hour away from Nice in the South of France where she spent all of her marriage to Germain (the sexy Frenchman). She always stands, in my imagination, behind him, in fact behind the sofa on which he is settled, comfortable and entitled. She paces there, in the background, thinking, plotting, devising. Occasionally in this oft-imagined scene, she reaches out to him and squeezes a shoulder or rubs his neck. *"Que veux-tu, mon amour?* Another drink? Let me get it for you."* This is all in preparation for her ask; the distraction, the pampering, the soothing will lull him, she hopes, into granting her that day's wish.

I grew up watching my mother make power plays in her own marriage, trying to get her way with my father. As an adult I see these plays for what they were: attempts at manipulation, similar in nature to Susanna's behind-the-scenes techniques. My mother would ask me to approach my father with a request or a suggestion as if it were coming from me, claiming *"Tu Daddy te escucha a ti."* She assumed, correctly, that my father, her husband, *"no le importa lo que yo quiero,"* and hoped he would listen to me. She complained out loud in front of the children, hoping to shame him into compliance with her wishes. My mother differed from Susanna only in that she was less pur- poseful, less systematic in her attempts to gain agency in her marriage; she was more spontaneous and less of a conscious strategist.

Importantly, my mother, unlike Susanna, grew up feeling cherished by both her parents. She did not feel excluded from that most fundamental of emotions, a mother's love. If anyone, it is only she, Susanna, who can know what happened to her psyche, to her soul, as a result of her mother's distancing herself from her: the pushing away, the denying of affection, the locking out of bedrooms. But I find the urge to be irresistible, and I must link that legendary childhood trauma to her later approach to her marriages, of which there are three in all, the last being the most successful or, perhaps more accurately, the least a failure. Did her mother, Tía Kitty, train her in emotional distance? Did this distance, in turn, drive Susanna to see marital relationships as transactional, even adversarial? Perhaps she believed her single source of agency to be that of the subservient: manipulation, distraction, deceit.

Today when I think of Susanna where she is at the moment, alone (Germain, her third and last husband, died a few years ago) in a house perched on a terraced hillside at the edge of the French Riviera, smoking her cigarettes, even now holding on to the provocative persona of a man's woman, I wonder if it was worth it to her. All of her scheming, her plotting, her machinations in a marriage unequal from the start. But, I also think, she grew up in a world where it was assumed men ruled. Some women accepted this assumption, others writhed under it, and still others, like my cousin, worked with it. I'm pretty sure Susanna thought she was making the best of her situation, married to a Frenchman, living by the sea on the Riviera. It was a given that she would use her "womanly wiles" to make her lot even better. But then again the word *wiles* makes me think of cunning, and cunning to me is an art used by the weak against the strong. Wile E. Coyote, always hungry, is desperate to catch the Road Runner but never succeeds. The Road Runner, on the other hand, with his freedom and his speed, remains blithely ignorant of the coyote and his desperation. Was it worth it, in the end? The massaging of shoulders, the filling of drinks, the silent, invisible scheming? Susanna today lives a solitary life, estranged from both her stepchildren and her own sons, the ever-present cigarettes her sole companions.

Thirty years later, I still cringe at my cousin's marital philosophy of masculine authority and womanly cunning, but at the same time I wouldn't argue against it with the same self-righteousness. I understand more how a Peruvian woman who came of age in the fifties and sixties, who grew up in a house saturated not by affection and love but by seeming coldness and rejection, could be proud of her covert bids for power. I still chafe, of course, at the gross inequities in our relationships that are about gender, at what defines a desirable woman and a coveted spouse, and ultimately at what made a wife plot and plan like some downstairs servant to have a say in how she lived her life. But it is a sad chafing.

Red Lipstick

(*Seattle, 1995*)

I read an article once, maybe twenty-five years ago, which made me uncomfortable. Although I read it after I'd come to understand that clothes can be armor, that choosing certain outfits and putting on makeup can be deliberate, thought-out acts of self-representation, I was left feeling torn between my instincts and my philosophy about women. In this article, a journalist wrote about interviewing female soldiers, her themes being femininity and feminism, the choices and sacrifices these women had to make in order to survive in their role as military in combat zones.

One soldier the writer interviewed was fighting, if memory serves me, in Eastern Europe somewhere. She was a fiercely proud warrior, disavowing any attraction to pretty clothes or nostalgia for mascara and blush. She wore her shapeless uniform with pride, and her thin hair scraped back from her face. The other soldier the writer interviewed was almost identical in style and looks to the first: she also wore the drab military green with its rough, canvas-like material, the unflattering pants, wide shirt, and thick boots. Her hair too, although thick and wavy, was pulled back, allowing no opportunity for an errant strand or curl to get into her eyes at precisely the wrong moment — when she had to set her rifle sights on a target, for instance, or use her peripheral vision to register approaching threats.

Yet for all their similarities, they were different in one key way: the second soldier's answers to questions about womanhood and femininity were given in a softer tone, more wistfully, less fiercely. The writer noticed in particular a tube of red lipstick this second soldier held in her possession, as if it were a good luck charm or an anchor to her past life, keeping her attached to her home and culture by the sheer force of its iconic status in the evolution of ideal femininity.

The reason I remember this article I read so long ago is that the writer admitted, almost regretfully, that she liked the second soldier better, the one whom some people would consider weak because she depended so heavily for solace, amid the fear and chaos of war, on a little tube of lipstick. And I was torn as I read about these two soldiers and then the writer's reluctant admittance, torn between the two examples of warrior womanhood: the "strong," committed warrior and her softer, weaker foil.

I had to admit to myself, to confess that in the depths of my own gut reactions I related to the lipsticked soldier. That I too would hate to dress every day in an ugly uniform, to pull my hair back, to have unlined eyes, invisible stubby lashes, pale undefined lips. I want to revel, when I feel like it, in prettiness. I want to seek beauty of every kind. I want to find it and focus on it and embrace it and live it.

It's only now, so many years later, that I don't see shame or weakness in wanting lipstick. It is the external world, our culture that—perversely—demands an allegiance to masculinist aesthetics in any attempt to defy patriarchy.

Breasts on the Baúl

(California, 1990)

One afternoon after school I walked into the entrance hall of my house. I'd just closed the front door behind me when I saw a package sitting on the baúl. *Baúl* means chest in Spanish, and in our house that baúl from India, made of dark wood inlaid with mother-of-pearl, had become the landing spot in the hallway for bags, purses, letters, or, as in this case, packages. The box was open and I could see nestled within it, among layers of bubble wrap and tissue paper, what looked like two water balloons. When I found my mother in the kitchen, I asked her about them. *"Ah,"* she said, *"son los implantes para tu prima."* They were silicone breasts.

An older cousin of mine wanted a larger chest. In her family, my aunt's family, the women have small chests—an A cup, or maybe at their largest, due to pregnancy and lactation, a B. The surgery could be done more easily and economically in Peru, so there was much negotiation between my mother and her sister, the mother of my breast implant-seeking cousin, to procure the actual silicone from the US and mail it to the plastic surgeon's office in Lima. It was strange to me to know that right there, in all their physicality, lay two liquid blobs, blobs that were destined to become part of my cousin's body, that were soon to be carefully placed on either side of her chest by a scalpel-wielding surgeon in order to enhance her desirability as a woman.

That sight—two plastic balloons in a cardboard box in my parents' entryway destined to become breasts inside a real live woman—still makes me time-travel back centuries, as far back to the queen of canny self-beautification, Cleopatra herself. And I wonder, thinking about her and her milk baths and honey masks, how she would react if she could look into the future, if she could see shimmering in front of her a hologram, like a moving tapestry on the wall, first the silicone bags on the baúl, then the operation wherein they are placed within the chest of my cousin, a young woman, to look better before the male gaze, to be more desirable to men, to become more completely, more perfectly, the sexual object. What would Cleopatra think? What would she feel?

I imagine, once she got over her shock at this unexpected sight, at the moving apparition with sound and in color, that she would be appalled by the monstrous and the grotesque of what she saw, by what she might read as a dystopic vision of unnecessary torture, suffering, and objectification, a slab of meat on a butcher block, plastic and silicone transforming the imperfect human into a sort of cyborg. Or, on the other hand, who's to say she wouldn't think it a magical procedure for self-enhancement and command her followers to find the magician capable of such transformation?

Then I fast-forward a millennium or two and imagine Jane Austen, she of social analysis, of gendered politicization, of acute observation of the commodification of the female body on the marriage market. What would she think if she could somehow see—perhaps in a dream she intuited as a message from the future—first the plastic-encased liquid on the wooden chest, then the bloody scalpel, the stretched muscle wall? What would she feel? Her heroines like to walk in the countryside, to write long letters, to engage in witty conversations, to dance at balls, to support beloved sisters, to marry worthy men. Would larger breasts allow them to more fully partake in these activities or more completely realize these goals? Would a perkier bosom enable them to most optimally achieve their idea of success?

I believe there can be no personal satisfaction, no pleasure or joy, in breast implants, except within patriarchal constructs. Women are not born dissatisfied with the size and shape of their breasts. They are not born sexualizing them in terms of appearance. With breast implants, there is pain and discomfort and cost and risk. There is money spent, there is pain in recovery, and there are scars forever. There is, always, risk of death, of numbness, of complications. What of this is joyful? What of this is pleasurable? At least a milk bath is relaxing, a honey mask soothing.

I grew up watching my aunt and my mother idolize the beautiful. For them, beauty is women's primary currency in this world. The smoothness of their skin, the delicacy of their features, the sexiness of their bodies. At the very least, a small nose and big breasts. If my mother and her sister needed a mantra or a brand, that would serve nicely: *Small Nose—Big Breasts! Small Nose—Big Breasts!* To that baseline they added petite ears, long glossy hair, pert bottoms. My mother sometimes talks about her decision *not* to have the surgeon who was stitching a cut on my forehead when I was seven pin back my elephantine ears at the same time. He did suggest it, after all. She wonders if she should regret that decision, but always ends up mollifying herself with the fact that my face grew into them and my hair over them. To this day my aunt bemoans the fact that she did not give one of her young cousins the money she needed for a nose job. This young cousin's identical twin was having one, but she herself didn't have the resources at the time. My aunt remains firm in the belief that her neglect to pay for the procedure is the reason this cousin never found a husband or started a family (as did her surgically small-nosed sister), and instead became a nun.

When I was younger I drank all this in. I embraced the idea that if you had the money and the surgeon, then what a miracle—instant beauty! I saw only the glamor of the rich who participated in these surgical rituals of beautification. But now that I'm older, I see the underbelly. I see what I imagine Jane Austen or even Cleopatra, with their virgin eyes, might see. Yet I continue to fantasize about tighter jawlines and lifted brows. In regards to cosmetic intervention, I feel like a Pushmi-Pullyu of Dr. Dolittle fame: fascination-aversion, fascination-aversion, fascination-aversion. Part of the fascination is that I've internalized what beauty is supposed to look like; I want to fit in; I want to "still" feel beautiful (read young) at fifty, at fifty-five. Part of the aversion is the gratuitous gore, the unnecessary cutting and suturing. Also, the guilt. Can a middle-aged feminist choose plastic surgery? *Should* a middle-aged feminist choose plastic surgery? Pushmi-Pullyu, back and forth the pendulum swings.

My cousin carried her new, larger breasts around for a few years before one day she didn't want to anymore: they were contracting, or leaking, or degrading, or all of the above, and her dream of a beauty sanctioned and revered by the male gaze paused in realization of the very real danger now embedded in her body. So she had them removed and slightly smaller, non-silicone ones put in their place. I never found out if these new implants, like their predecessors, ever made a pit stop at my parents' house to spend a night or two on the baúl.

Leda

(California, 1991)

I sit in the lecture hall dedicated this Saturday to the taking of the Graduate Record Examination. There are no voices; there is no conversation, lecturing, chitchat, or laughter. The room is quiet except for the rustle of pages, the clearing of throats and the occasional cough, the ticking of the large white clock, even the soft scrape of lead on paper. The questions are multiple choice, and there are more than two hundred of them on poetry and drama, literary theory and the history of language, as well as the essay, novel, and short story. Based on excerpts, some of the questions are analytical, asking me to examine a passage of prose or poetry and think about meaning and language, while others are factual, asking me to identify the characteristics of literary movements, name a work on the basis of a critical comment or style, or know an author from the content provided.

I'm reading quickly, my brain divided. Part of my mind scans the words, the lines, the paragraphs; another part pays attention to what might direct me to the correct answer; and yet another wrestles with itself, continuously tamping down the anxiety about taking the test, remembering all I've memorized, paying close attention to avoid getting distracted. And, simultaneously, there are the fingers clutching the yellow pencil, the bent head, the stiffening neck, the repositioning of the legs, the quick glances at the clock.

Many quotes are boring and historical and feel dead to me: Gilgamesh, Beowulf, Chaucer, Boswell. At others my interest perks up, mostly those from women: Austen and Hong Kingston, Eliot and Morrison. And then—*STOP*—all systems down, on hold, paused. The eyes cease their forced march down the page; the hand forgets the pencil it still holds to rest on the desk; the clock, the questions, the waiting empty bubbles are forgotten, suddenly insignificant.

A sudden blow: the great wings beating still
Above the staggering girl, her thighs caressed
By the dark webs, her nape caught in his bill,
He holds her helpless breast upon his breast.

There on the page, quite abruptly, is beauty embodied, majesty and grace represented, sorrow and awe rendered readable.

How can those terrified vague fingers push
The feathered glory from her loosening thighs?
And how can body, laid in that white rush,
But feel the strange heart beating where it lies?

Moments like these are hard to describe for a reader ambushed as I am, and language fails me, the teller of the tale.

A shudder in the loins engenders there
The broken wall, the burning roof and tower
And Agamemnon dead.

Is it enough to say that time seemed to stand still, that only the words stood out, that the beauty and the violence they inspired were all that existed in that single, sustained moment? Perhaps not. So let me try again. If I were the protagonist of a movie, let's say, then this would be the scene where all sounds—the scratch of pencils and the flutter of pages, the squeak of chairs and the sighs of examinees—die down, and the camera zooms in closer and closer toward the words on the page. Within this laser focus, every letter of every word is clearly delineated and boldly printed, its edges razor sharp.

> *Being so caught up,*
> *So mastered by the brute blood of the air,*
> *Did she put on his knowledge with his power*
> *Before the indifferent beak could let her drop?*

As if to a sudden blow, my psyche reacts to the poem, to its style and content, to the images it conjures like magic.

I wasn't prepared. I hadn't come across that poem in all my studying, throughout all my reading and memorizing and note-taking. I didn't have a clue who had written those words. I don't even know today if I guessed correctly and filled the bubble next to William Butler Yeats. I could only read and reread the short poem, careless of the time it took from completing the exam, mesmerized, hypnotized, drugged as I was by its beauty. Although I wasn't aware of it then, ahead of me lay guilt and confusion for the way I was drawn to these words that spoke so compellingly of force and coercion, of violence and rape.

And yet I knew even as I first read it that something disturbed me about the poem. I couldn't articulate it at the time, inexperienced as I was and caught up in the poem's lyrical power. But today, three decades later, I know what to look for, which questions to ask. Why, for example, is it titillating for a woman to copulate with an animal? Leda, a mortal—raped by a swan. Pasiphae, a goddess—breeds with a bull. Belle, the loyal daughter in the age-old fairy tale—kisses a beast. I take on the shame for my gender. I take on the humiliation of the feminized body. I take on the repulsion. It's not sexy or titillating or edgy to me. I am Leda, Pasiphae, Belle.

What also bothers me: Christianity has the New Testament, the text that is the Word, sacred and inviolable. It has Mary as Leda, the Holy Spirit as Zeus. But Mary's rape has been sanitized, emasculated in a sense, with the Phallus disembodied. The coupling of woman and creature, of Leda and the Swan, where the physical moment is central, has been siphoned away from Mary and the Holy Spirit. Christ's conception, called immaculate, has not, however, been purified. An angel appears before Mary, tall, male, and powerful, as well as immortal and divine. He tells her what will happen. He does not ask. Putting myself in Mary's place, how could I refuse? There is no option. The act remains coercive.

One image of Mary has stayed with me since childhood. It may have come from the shrine to the Virgin that stood in the corner of my backyard in Manila. Her statue smiled serenely; dressed in pastels, she seemed to exude acceptance. It may have come from the Catholic catechism at the local church in Northern California after school, where, bored with the text, I perused the illustrations of the Mother of God found in our booklets. She was invariably depicted as calm, her expression mild, with no frowns marring her forehead, no downturned mouth making ugly her youthful countenance. It may have come from my missionary middle school in Quito, where I was taught, over and over, the details of Christ's conception. In the King James version, Mary is an innocent mortal, picked by God to bear his only son.

The Angel Gabriel appears, snowy-winged and clothed in white. "The Holy Ghost shall come upon thee," he tells Mary, "and the power of the Highest shall overshadow thee . . . that holy thing which shall be born of thee shall be called the Son of God." Despite the language of domination—*power*, *come upon*, *overshadow*, even *thing*—both catechism class and missionary school focused on the honor bestowed upon Mary in this moment, the privilege of being the chosen one. The possibility of coercion or violence, that subtext so clear to me now, was never acknowledged.

I think about my rape, if one can "own" a rape—for that was what it was, in the end, no matter how much I later contextualized it (I knew the man, I spent the night with him) or how much I rationalized its inevitability (we'd done almost everything but actual intercourse, I was sleeping next to him naked). But I, like Leda, experienced the sudden blow; for me it was the wakening in the dark to a force above me and a pressure on me, relentless, refusing to leave me alone, to stop, no matter how I struggled beneath the weight. But there never was a mitigating mystery in a beating heart I could not help but hear and feel. I was too preoccupied with *my* heart, my heart that was beating frantically, angrily, impotently.

Both the Greek legend of Leda and the Swan and the Christian myth of Mary and the Immaculate Conception feature the all-important seed—the shudder of the loins on which pivots the course of history. It is the male energy, semen and seed, that creates, and the woman, whether Leda or Mary, becomes peripheral to the real action, a pawn for the determining force. When I awoke because of a sudden blow to my trustful sleep, when I found myself trapped under a man's thrusting body, was there a subsequent shudder of his loins within my own? Thinking back, I try to shed light onto the darkness that is that time, to illuminate the dimness of my memory. At first I can't remember. But then I can: I wasn't on the pill, and he didn't use a condom. I know because I counted the days until my period was due.

This was the first poem that ever captivated me in any way, and it did so utterly and completely. Until that moment poems to me were boring, at best clever for an instant and then forgotten. Now I know I had neither the right poems nor, still immature, the necessary patience. But this short poem arrested me, forced me to pay attention, and more, made me fall under its spell and enter a world I'd never thought existed, a world where a violent history is rendered exalted, where rape is made sublime.

Despite all these thoughts and all this time, over thirty years, whenever I reread *Leda and the Swan* I'm still moved. It could be that I can't help but borrow for myself some of the power of that legendary history, of the passion and the tragedy of lust, war, and conquest evoked in its narrative. It could be that I simply cannot resist the urgent beauty of the words.

There Is a Way Out

(*California, 1991*)

I'm at a local playground that is small and fenced in, exclusive. This playground lies at the center of an expansive park that, preserved by money from concrete and development, exists in the middle of an affluent neighborhood known for its magnificent nature—trails and hills, creeks and reservoirs—as well as its schools, rich with funding and investment.

Years later, looking back, I will recognize a magical quality to the privacy, the quiet, the protectiveness of that space. Women and children. Mothers with sons and daughters. Nannies and babysitters. Girls and women and young boys. No men. A large skeleton key is needed to get in, to enter that space and access that playground with its swings, sand, and seesaw. There is another protective layer, like a girdle, besides the high wooden fence: the leaf-laden and pine-needled trees that grow close, tall bodyguards, boughs reaching across to shade a corner, a bench, a sand pit.

I'm at the playground with my employer, the mother of the two children I care for as a part-time job before starting a graduate program—taking them to the park and staying with them on an occasional weekend evening, feeding them, changing them, reading to them. Their mother is a kind of role model to me—beautiful, poised, and elegant. Dark of eyes and hair, thin and fashionable, this employer, this mother, represents what I want to be. Whenever I'm near her, I become acutely aware of my kinky hair, big ears, and low-budget wardrobe.

This mother, my employer, met me here at the park and has decided to stay for a few minutes before taking her children back home. We sit on a wooden bench together, side by side, chatting companionably, as we watch the children play, sometimes getting up to dust off a child who has fallen or interrupting the flow of our conversation to dispense encouragement, caution, or praise.

Our talk turns to the subject that has weighed on my mind in recent months. Should I commit to my boyfriend of six years? Should I, as my mother advises, either marry or break up? Is it true that staying with him after "all these years" is a waste of my time, time that is precious because I am a young woman in my twenties whose primary goal, again according to my mother, is to find a husband?

Later, when I'm married and for the first few months homesick, insecure, and experiencing seasonal affective disorder in my new home in gloomy Seattle, I will realize the depth of my mother's chauvinism. Because my mother, born and raised in Peru, socialized in the particular and potent patriarchy of South America, says to me in response to my unhappiness, to my desperate search for solutions, perhaps even for an escape, that at least I will be *una divorciada y no una solterona*—at least, even if I leave my husband, I won't bear the stigma of spinster-hood, the indignity of being an old maid.

That day at the park, however, when still unmarried and not yet relocated to another state, climate, and subculture, my mother's pressure affected me. Even as my mind rejected the implication that my primary goal as a young woman and a daughter was to marry well in order to secure social and financial protection, my emotions—my guilt, my sense of responsibility to my mother and even to my future children—responded to that imperative.

Portrait of a Feminist

I ask my employer, the mother sitting next to me in the hush of this autumnal afternoon, in the quiet of the little island created by the fence, the locked door, and the surrounding band of trees, "Should I get married? I mean, what if it's the wrong decision? How do I even know if he's *the one*?"

My employer thinks for a moment, gazing at the dappled sunlight on the sand, at the partially buried shovels and trucks and dolls, then answers. "You know, I don't think there has to be a 'one.' Look at me—I'm happily married, but sometimes I still think about my exes. I even dream about them."

"You do? So many of my friends talk about not having any doubts because they're marrying their best friend. But I feel like getting married is like doors closing on me. Like I'll be stuck on this one narrow path."

"I get that," she says, "but look, I was more like you. I wasn't one hundred percent sure . . . I had some doubts. And I don't regret my choice even though I wonder about the past sometimes."

There's a pause as we each contemplate this idea, this notion that maybe marriage doesn't have to be a tight casket, a windowless room, that it can be flexible enough to allow space, at least psychically, for what or who was *not*—for, in the end, the path not taken.

"Well," my employer continues, "I think you should just do it. Get married. You'll never know unless you do it. As long as you don't have children, you can always get a divorce."

I know now it's because of this—because of that singular idea, then so radical to me—that I remember this moment in time so vividly: on the bench, in the park, babysitting for pocket money, between college and graduate school, between singleness and coupledom. It was as if, at that moment, the claustrophobia I felt at the thought of choosing one person to marry—of committing legally, officially, on paper, to one man, one family, one life—lifted in an instant. I felt a sense of freedom I'd never before felt when thinking about marriage. The sense of oppression that always accompanied the idea of an engagement, a wedding, or a marriage certificate lifted along with my assumption of the irrevocability of the marriage vow. I could always get a divorce! There was *a way out*.

I did get married, and I'm still married. I'm still married three decades after I heard that advice, advice that might seem obvious to others, especially today, but that struck me with the impact of a lightning bolt—illuminating the future, freeing my choices.

My former employer, however, the mother at the park next to whom I sat that long ago day on a bench, the mother who wore white linen and black denim, who adorned her slim wrists with Cartier gold, whose dark hair was always smooth and shiny and soft, that mother—the wise woman to my ingénue, the mentor to my protégé, the teacher to my student—is divorced. After three children and thirty years. After a son married, a daughter relocated to Italy, and the youngest gone to college. Divorced, but only after her children left home. Only when any damage to her son and daughters would be minimized by their adulthood, by the agency that comes with the maturity to make their own choices. Whenever I think about this divorce, about my mentor-employer taking this particular way out despite her advice so long ago depending on a state of childlessness, I think about the timing. And it all makes sense.

Sunglasses

(*California, 1992*)

*I*t was a day trip to Santa Cruz. An easy two hours, since we all lived in Marin County or San Francisco. We were four on this Saturday outing: my friend, his friend Raj, Raj's girlfriend, and me. This wasn't a double date, though. The boy was the only male friend I've ever had, and by friend I mean someone with whom I felt comfortable within seconds of meeting up, with whom I analyzed affairs of the heart and dissected sexual exploits (mostly his) past and present, with whom outings and clubs and restaurants had that added frisson of interest because we shared a sympathy of minds.

My memories of those days, as a teenager and into my twenties, are anchored by images, as if a fashion designer's expert sketches, of what I wore. My outfits act as bookmarks signaling the gateway to further recall, sometimes in technicolor rewind, of an event.

I remember exactly what I was wearing on that day, the Saturday of the Santa Cruz outing. Prone to monochromatic looks, I wore an off-white T-shirt tied at the waist, off-white jeans, and even off-white sandals. But what I will never forget are the shoulder pads. Obsessed with the broad shoulders of the *Vogue* layouts that featured models with wide shoulders further accentuated by pads, I had acquired a set of large curved ones to offset the unfortunate narrowness of my own shoulders. With

the help of stick-on Velcro, I attached them easily to my tops
and T-shirts, completing a look I coveted from magazine shoots
and celebrity styles. When perusing photographs from that time
period, they strike me as overly large—my eye has readjusted
since then—and what comes to mind today is the massive bulk
of the football uniform. I wonder if that was part of the appeal
for me: the illusion of strength, a uniform that suggested a kind
of power I didn't have.

All of that day in Santa Cruz besides my outfit—who drove
what car, if I sat in the front or the back, when we arrived, where
and what we ate, if we walked on the boardwalk at all, what time
we left—has faded from my memory, has disappeared from the
filed scenes and images in my mind, except for a single moment.
The boy and I stand on a bridge that spans a smallish river. Raj
and his girlfriend have wandered off somewhere, and so the boy
and I find ourselves alone for a few minutes. The bridge is a
roughly finished pedestrian bridge, the wood of the railing
scratchy on my bare forearms as I lean on it to look over into the
water below. Although the river moves slowly, with an amble
rather than a sprint toward the ocean a mile or two farther south,
light still reflects off its rolling undulations, and the soft shimmers
that gleam here and there attract my eye. It would be easy to
render the scene before us in abstract, the grasses and trees
flanking the river two green strokes of paint, the river a blue-
green smudge in between, the sky a simple blue canopy. But I
recall it impressionistically, with a bit more detail. I see the roots
of the trees that crowd together to feed from the continuously
flowing water, the grass and shrubs that compete for real estate
on the muddy bank. To the sides, beyond the walls of green, are
buildings and roads and street signs, human life going on as
backdrop. I can hear the melded sounds of car engines, shouts
from the boardwalk rides, the strident calls of seagulls.

The boy stands close to me, and we talk as we gaze at the

river, at the dark depths under the dancing of the light, for we cannot see past the surface of the water. I feel the warmth and weight of the boy next to me, close although we aren't touching, the wooden floorboards of the bridge creaking whenever we shift positions.

His warmth blends with the warmth of the thick railing, a dark timber that has been absorbing the California sun for the past several hours. We're in the calm eye at the center of the storm, he and I, just for a few minutes cocooned from the everyday chaos of life that never stops. Side by side, we lean on the railing, looking at the river as it flows, slowly yet steadily, toward the ocean, its path predetermined. We're conversing, easily, satisfyingly, as we usually do, as we always do. We're used to analyzing people and situations, to gossiping and judging and planning, the both of us, together. It feels frank and open between us, an effortless communication that never fails to gratify.

What the boy doesn't realize during our conversation, however, is that there's an undercurrent of melancholy in my side of the exchange, of low spirits in my mood, regardless of how normal and cheerful I strive to appear. I feel this melancholy as tangibly as I see the river flowing beneath me. But the boy doesn't know. He doesn't know because I haven't told him. I haven't told him I am to be married, and soon—next week as a matter of fact, in just a few days.

It's curious that although I feel so comfortable with the boy that I confide in him embarrassing incidents and personal insights, I stop at telling him about my plans to marry, a major milestone in any person's life. It could have to do with the speed with which the plans have been made between my long-term boyfriend and me, between us and our families. It has been in the air all summer, this pressure to finally "do" something with our relationship—either break up or, as my mother has long advised, get married. Both of us overthinkers, it took a month of heavy-duty negotiations on the phone, of listing the pros and cons, in order to come to an agreement. Romantic, at this point, we are not. But the ball has landed on the court of marriage; the scales have tipped toward a life together.

I know I talked about my boyfriend with the boy, and he knew the outline if not all the details of our relationship. We talked about so much, he and I, it was almost as if we were best girlfriends. Yet I must have remained silent on the subject of the negotiations, of my ambivalence, my reluctance to leave home, family, and friends to move to another state, one alien to me in its damp climate and indifferent welcome.

The boy was one of the friends I dreaded leaving. He had come to represent a side of my character, in my young adulthood, hitherto unknown even to me. One that felt a sense of freedom in bypassing the rules and regulations, both spoken and unspoken, for a daughter of a Peruvian mother, the girlfriend of a Middle Easterner, the future daughter-in-law of strictly non-American parents. Mostly vicariously, but sometimes simultaneously, I'd been able with the boy to experience rule-breaking: driving too fast on roads too curvy; analyzing his father's porn videos; drinking wine on lonely sand dunes that faced westward to the open sea; taking a secret road trip to LA to be his plus-one at a wedding. The prospect of leaving California for Seattle—of leaving my family, my mother especially, of leaving my friends, including the boy—was making me sad. I couldn't explain it to him because I had chosen, consciously or subconsciously, not to tell him until the very last minute. I wanted to extend the feeling of freedom, of having a companion in fun and spontaneity. I wanted the Santa Cruz outing to be like all our other outings. And I thought I could contain my melancholy and keep it away from him, that I could prevent my mood from tainting the day.

What came next, on that bridge spanning a river in an oceanside town on a warm Saturday, was a tussle of sorts.

Maybe a wrestling match in miniature. A struggle of some kind. Over what? I can't remember. He was bigger and stronger than me, so any fight was in jest, of course. What did he want from me? To take from me? Now that I think about it, I believe it was the sunglasses. My sunglasses. They were the most expensive sunglasses I'd ever owned. Because I'd needed to save money to buy them, they meant time and effort and discipline on my part. Designer sunglasses in a tortoiseshell finish from Neiman Marcus rather than Longs Drugs, I thought they complemented my creamy off-white ensemble admirably. And I didn't want to relinquish them to the boy at that moment. Perhaps I didn't want to face the glare of the sun. Or I felt he didn't have a reason valid enough to necessitate the effort of taking them off, with much care, squinting as I handed them to him. Maybe I didn't want them to get smudged in the exchange. Or I didn't want him to try them on and stretch them in the process. I can't remember today the exact nature of my jealous guardianship over that first pair of designer sunglasses. But I recall the tussle it resulted in. And I recall, with precise clarity, the result of that tussle.

The sunglasses fell. They slipped from my face and down into the river. In a second they were gone—never to be recovered, lost forever.

My reaction was just as instantaneous, my irritation at the loss immediate. I was angry. And I directed my anger toward the boy. It had to be his fault because I wanted to blame someone, and he was the closest and thus the handiest. What was also lost at that moment was my self-control, the reserve I'd maintained all day in order to protect the boy from catching the melancholia from me, that sense of sorrowfulness for what would soon be left behind. The gates were opened, the dam breached. The reality of the real world, of the imminent end of an era in my own life, broke through the shell I'd created around me and the boy and rushed in. My mood, heretofore pushed down, hidden from the rest of the party, was exposed. I acted irritated—angry and annoyed—like a sulky child. But in reality, I was sad.

Aghast, the boy apologized profusely. Innocent of my future plans, he focused on the loss of the sunglasses themselves and offered to replace them, or to give me money. But I, knowing the real reason for my distress, as well as the fact that it wasn't really his fault—he hadn't meant for the sunglasses to fall into the river—refused his offers and his comfort. Instead, I looked silently over the bridge and at the river, toward the spot where I imagined the glasses had landed, with a small splash, to be swallowed entirely by the depths of the dark water.

I never saw the boy again. One of the last times we spoke on the phone was the morning of my rushed wedding at the local civic center, when I told him I was moving away.

Part Three

MATURATION

Slutty Boots

(Seattle, 1992)

he first day at my graduate school in Seattle was muted, brushed with shades of gray. The opaque lake nearby, the dull firs everywhere, the overcast sky above, they each conspired with the campus buildings, solid old brick or Communist-bloc concrete, to ensure a forbidding landscape. The students, almost all clad in Gortex or Patagonia, fleece and denim, suited the bleak campus. I was used to California, to the dependability of the sun and blue sky, the soft greens of valley oaks near bright, poppy orange, ferns next to lavender and Mexican sage. I was used to my undergraduate campus in Berkeley with its different ethnicities—Black and white and Asian and Indian and Latino, styles of clothes—athletic and bohemian and preppy and punk, identities—artist and international, frat boy and sorority girl, science nerd and jock. I was used to the students who studied and sunbathed and people-watched outside, encouraged by warmth and light.

But here students scurried from class to class, building to building, library to cafeteria and back, hoods up and faces averted from mist, drizzle, or wind. Among people with piercings and tattoos, women with cropped hair and men with shaggy locks, everyone in the uniform of jeans and flannel and Doc Martens, I felt strangely conventional. My clothes were fitted, my mouth lipsticked red, my hair long in black curls. In my new school and state I felt, with my designer boots, makeup, and painted nails, the odd one out—too colorful and exotic, yet at the same time too conservative, too mainstream.

For days after I arrived at my new home, I refused to unpack the car except for a toothbrush and pajamas. It soothed me to see the familiar Volkswagen Jetta from the kitchen window, sitting in the driveway like a loyal valet, its backseat crammed with boxes of clothes and books. It was only after a week that I could empty the car, putting my Levi's, leather boots, and denim jackets away in the closet of the master bedroom, the one I shared with my new husband.

My husband was in a different graduate program, in what felt like a separate world. His fellow medical residents were all men and all white, Christian, and heterosexual. Their wives spoke longingly of homes in Georgia and Texas and Boston, to which they looked forward, after doing their time supporting their husbands, to returning. They couldn't wait to quit their jobs, buy mansions in gated communities, get pregnant, take up the piano, join the country club. Although their aspirations were alien to my own, I see now that we were the same in our hunger for happiness from a limited buffet, as any of the few choices available to us as wives came with compromise if not sacrifice. But I didn't realize any of this then; I simply experienced an alienation that felt like loneliness, and an isolation that felt like melancholy.

One evening, six months after we were married, my husband and I went out with two of these residents and their wives. My husband made the initial introductions to the couple I didn't know: Parker, serious, dark-haired, and spectacled, quietly good-looking in a way that evoked Clark Kent, and his wife Pamela, big-eyed and tiny-nosed, wearing a turtleneck, delicate jewelry, and a hairband, her look a mixture of Bambi and sorority sister.

As I approached Parker to shake his hand, I noticed his

eyes flick over me, from kinky hair to black boots. His facial expression, just a moment before open and ready, changed. I sensed disgust, a sort of repulsion, at my person, my style, my look. In a flash I saw what he saw: unruly hair, mannish jacket, tight leggings, slutty boots—and instantly regretted my outfit. Just a half-hour earlier, I'd stood in front of the closet trying to decide what to wear. After much inner debate, I chose what for me was a fairly daring outfit, but one I thought edgy and sophisticated. Although the cotton tee under the cropped jacket covered my hips, I'd hesitated before making my decision. Now, standing in front of this man, I couldn't help it—I was embarrassed, mortified even. I felt vulgar and gaudy, a slash of scarlet in a palette of pastels. I wanted to run home to change into something more discreet, more appropriate, or turn back the clock and put on a different outfit in the first place, an outfit that was less flashy, less, as my mother would say, *llamativo*.

My Peruvian mother, I knew, would have agreed with my urge to go home and change. I grew up studying photographs taken in 1950s Lima of my mother on the beach wearing a simple black bathing suit, hair coiffed, a long string of creamy pearls around her neck. In San Francisco during the sixties, she eschewed the new fashion of bell bottoms and tunics, of beads and bare feet and dreadlocks, in favor of silk shantung sheathes, pointy kitten heels, and straightened hair. My mother vowed that I, her baby girl born two months before the Summer of Love, would never set foot anywhere near Haight-Ashbury.

I've always held an image in my mind of a moment that occurred a year or so before I got married: my mother pulls, frustrated, at the side of a clingy knit dress I refuse to replace with a less revealing one before an evening in the city. My mother wanted her daughter to always be classy or *fina*, never tacky or *huachafa*. She tried to tame my wild frizzy hair, starting in my tweens and continuing throughout my teens. At my mother's prompting, I endured hours in large plastic rollers under the dome of a dryer to achieve a smoother look. I spent entire afternoons in a salon chair with toxic chemicals brushed into my hair in attempts at permanent glossiness. I cried once, trying to hide the tears I couldn't help, as two stylists tackled my knots, their brushes pulling at my scalp from both sides of my head. All efforts failed. My hair was impervious to any attempts at taming or control.

In that split second of introduction to my husband's colleague, the old sense of inadequacy rose inside me. Under Parker's gaze, I became Cinderella reduced to rags at the ball, exposed as an imposter.

Later, at the restaurant, I was prepared for the boredom that inevitably made up a large part of any gathering of two or more residents. I was accustomed, in these kinds of settings, to the course of the conversation being dictated by my husband and his colleagues. Medical talk dominated. So on this night I was pleasantly surprised when, during appetizers, Parker turned his attention to me. "So what do you do?"

I told him I attended the English graduate program at the university.

"Ah," he responded, carefully spreading butter on a piece of bread, "isn't that place full of *lesbians*?"

Here was another value judgment, another criticism, another suggestion of contempt.

Immediately on the defensive, I glared at him, but only inwardly, thinking, *How dare he generalize like that? How dare he try to belittle me?* Out loud I said, "Um . . . *no*. There are plenty of heterosexuals in my department. And what if it *was* 'full' of lesbians?"

The conversation around us died down as the others at the table picked up on the combative undercurrent of our exchange. My husband changed the subject. Before the meal was over, however, during dessert, Parker pointed at his cheesecake and urged me to help myself.

Grateful for what I took as a gesture of good faith, maybe even an apology, I accepted his invitation and ate from his offered plate. "This is really good!" I made sure to say, thinking I should reward him for his conciliatory effort.

This friendliness, this reaching out, this intimacy between us manifested in the sharing of food across a table, lulled me into a false sense of security. Later, after we said "good night . . . it was nice meeting you . . . we should do this again . . . oh yes, definitely" to Parker and his wife, my husband and I accompanied the other couple, Dennis and Sophia, to their small student apartment. Sitting on the secondhand sofa and garage-sale chairs, we rehashed the evening, discussing the differences between the four of us on the one hand and Parker and Pamela on the other. Parker seemed to have one purpose: to work tirelessly so he could get back to his church and his community and join a lucrative practice. His wife, meanwhile, seemed to have one role: to support him. She worked at a respectable but low-paying job in administration, clearly a transitional position, while waiting for their real life, the one with money and status, to begin back in their hometown.

Pamela was small and delicately pretty, with peaches-and-cream skin, long, soft brown hair, safe clothes. She accented her blue eyes with brown mascara and her lips with pink gloss. Her hair wasn't bushy or her skin brown, her height wasn't ungainly or her identity "ethnic." She seemed the perfect wife for Parker—someone who reflected him quietly, in the background, in no way *llamativa*. She hadn't said much at the restaurant, picking at her salad instead and seeming always to defer to her husband.

That night after dinner, Sophia and Dennis told us about the time they'd been invited to Parker and Pamela's apartment for Thanksgiving and Parker had criticized the turkey, humiliating his wife in front of the guests. They also spoke about the time he announced, regarding the husbands' surgical specialty, "Women can't do this job — it's too physical."

Then the phone rang. Dennis picked up the receiver. "Hello?"

It was Parker, who launched into a loud attack on me, the wife of his colleague, whom he had just met. He criticized me for my clothes, my personality, and my "radical feminism." Much of what he said was audible to the rest of us in the cramped living room. Dennis got off the phone as quickly as he could, but not before Parker realized his faux pas — we were all there, on the other side of the phone, getting the gist, if not every detail, of his diatribe.

What followed was an odd, uneasy peacemaking attempt. The next day Parker contacted my husband, "man to man." He apologized profusely to him, stating that he misspoke concerning my graduate program and that he didn't mean to insult me or offend him. It seemed a poor patch-up job, but my husband accepted the raggedy olive branch to maintain civil relations with his colleague in what was a small community of residents. Parker simultaneously sent his wife to apologize to me. I felt forced to accept her invitation to lunch, and a few days later sat at a seafood restaurant watching Pamela eat her Cobb salad (dressing on the side, no bread thank you), while I had fish with rice and plenty of bread to begin with. As we ate, Pamela awkwardly, dutifully, tried to explain away her husband's behavior.

I had accepted this lunch invitation because I felt pressured to — not by my husband but by my aversion to open confrontation and unresolved conflict. I wanted the bad feelings to go away. The only way to accomplish that, it appeared, was to pretend, to gloss over the hurt and outrage, to comfort Pamela with a series of *that's okays* and *I understands*.

In the end, relations between us did seem to smooth over, at least on the surface, and Parker was ever after extra friendly to my husband and extra polite to me. We met a handful of times after that evening and before the dispersal of the residents to different corners of the country upon graduation, albeit exclusively at formal functions where the pretense of civility was easy and superficial manners structured into a predetermined script. But I never wore that outfit again.

Faith

(Greensboro, 1994)

My friend since middle school had just given birth to a little girl—sweet and white and delicate. I spent a fair amount of money to buy Sarah's new baby an expensive dress, all creamy silk and precise embroidery with little puffed sleeves, like an outfit for a tiny Anne of Green Gables. Sarah was so pleased with this dress that she had her daughter wear it to the christening. Now that we have drifted apart, and haven't spoken for decades, the fact that Sarah chose my dress for her firstborn's christening comforts me—I feel like a fairy godmother who, once upon a time, was allowed to leave a gift.

Sarah and her husband lived in North Carolina. When I was scheduled to give a paper at a university conference in Greensboro, I naturally stayed with them.

I stood out in Greensboro. My fitted jacket and leather boots, my dangly gold earrings and long black hair prompted my friend to joke, "People must think you're our fancy nanny!" I knew that Sarah meant to compliment her visiting friend's coastal urbanity, but still her comment sat uneasily with me. My friend was a white so pale that, before she put on makeup, both eyebrows and eyelashes blended with her skin, rendering them virtually invisible. Military-handsome, her husband had intense blue eyes, a square jaw, and dark blond hair worn in a tight crew cut. The little baby, still too young to have been marked by the sun, was even paler than Sarah. I, definitely brown in comparison, felt oddly exoticized by my friend's teasing about the way we might look to strangers. As a Latina in Greensboro I was in between—in between races and skin tones, in between white and black.

The day before my presentation, I practiced for it by reading my paper out loud, in a separate room from Sarah but not, I sensed, totally out of earshot. My paper analyzed a futuristic novel in which lesbians of color relocate to Peru to establish an inclusive community. As I methodically articulated the graduate school jargon, careful to pace myself, I wondered if my friend was listening, and what she could be thinking about terms like *queer*, *abject*, *transmigratory*, and *ontological*. The ideas the words represented must feel vaguely threatening, I thought to myself as I read to the empty room, or at least somewhat repugnant to a person like Sarah, a woman who left graduate school because she couldn't stomach the debates, a woman who lived in the superiority of believing in the right god and belonging to the dominant race, a woman secure in owning her first marital home, nurturing her family, and attending her church.

On Sunday we went to the morning service at the local Church of Christ where Sarah and her husband were members. The building was plain and white, old-fashioned in architecture, cold and simple in interior, with narrow windows that let in little natural light. We sat in a row on a wooden pew for the singing and the sermon. Everyone in the church, with the exception of myself, was white. In Greensboro, it seemed, Black and brown people had their own churches, their own congregations, their own services.

Having been to church with Sarah in the past, I was prepared for her husband to lead the singing because I knew he had a strong voice. I knew too that in their sect all leadership positions were reserved for men; women and girls listened to the sermon and the prayers, only speaking to recite a prayer or sing as a group, both under the guidance of a male leader.

I couldn't help myself on our way home. In the car alone with my friend, I felt compelled to bring up the sexism of the service, the chauvinism inherent to the practices and philosophies of the Church of Christ.

"I just don't understand *why* women can't talk or lead the singing or the prayers. You can't really believe that women are inferior to men?"

I don't remember exactly how Sarah answered me. This was, after all, an old argument between us, a tired debate. She always went back to the New Testament—where the newly Christian Paul, with the fervor of the converted, instructs the Christian community in Corinthia to keep their women quiet because their voices, their opinions, don't have a place in a public forum of worship. Instead, a wife should take any issue— any problem, question, or solution—to her husband as head of the family; if *he* deems it worthy, he will bring it up at church.

I was familiar with this passage of the Bible because it was Sarah's mother who had, years prior, sent me for proof of God's silencing women to St. Paul's letter. Despite the intervening years, I still couldn't accept this, even from the Bible itself. I'd begun to think more critically of history and who writes what, when, and why. I doubted the Bible as sacred text.

Our discussion became heated. Hurt, Sarah blurted out, "But this is my religion, my *faith* you're criticizing!"

Hearing this, I struggled to defend my position. I tried to explain that my feminism, as a way of organizing the world, of defining humanity by emphasizing connections and compassion and equality, was as important to me as Sarah's Christianity was to her.

Only now, so many years later, do I know what it was I was trying to say: Feminism is *my* faith.

Her Name Was Tessa

(Seattle, 2001)

*H*er name was Tessa and she was my student.

For two years I taught at a small Jesuit university. One of my classes, an introduction to rhetoric and composition, was mandatory. It was mandatory for every first-year student to take, and for me, as newer faculty, to teach. But I didn't love to teach writing; I didn't even like it. What I loved to teach was literature. And my passion was feminism. Embryonic when I acted as self-appointed referee for my parents' power struggles, still inchoate in high school where the nuns lived committed to *veritas*, in infancy at university where I discovered the language and activism for social justice, maturing in graduate school as I learned the nuances of that language and the possibilities of that activism, feminism—its discourse, philosophy, practice, and identity—was always my driving force.

The question I asked at the start of every semester: *Who here is a feminist?*

I always felt disappointment, and surges of frustration, at the results of these informal polls. Rarely did any girl's hand go up, at once, with confidence and assurance. Instead, after some hesitancy, two or three hands would rise, with their owners all the while looking around, self-conscious, hoping not to be in too obvious a minority. These were also the days when no boy's hand ever moved, however minutely, even for a nanosecond, to claim feminism for its owner.

"Do you realize," I'd ask, struggling against stridency, "that less than a hundred years ago women weren't allowed to attend universities? Or vote? Or sit on juries? That it was just a couple of decades ago that women in some states were allowed to have their own credit card?" I wanted to shock the young faces in front of me into recognition, outrage, or at least a degree of gratitude. "It's because of feminists who sacrificed reputation, family, sometimes their lives, that you're all sitting here, that I'm standing here, that I drove here, that I voted in the last presidential election!"

I sensed in my students, the boys and the girls, a lack of investment and a lack of concern, a general lack of interest in the entire subject of feminism—what equality, regardless of sex or gender, could mean for women and men, for mothers, fathers, sisters, brothers, girlfriends, boyfriends, future sons, future daughters. For themselves. They didn't seem to care.

I don't remember if Tessa raised her hand in response to my question. I don't think she did. If she had, her quiet demeanor, her dark, pulled-back hair, her serious expression—they would have stuck with me from the beginning. But they didn't.

Because I was determined to teach writing in a way that would make it interesting to me, and also, hopefully, open some of my students' minds to the transformative potential in feminism, I decided to teach writing through the analysis of stories by women and about women, stories about the gendered struggle to self-express, to be heard and seen, to seize agency and resist patriarchy, to create alternative ways of thinking and being.

Her name was Sylvia, meaning "forest." Young Sylvia found peace only when she moved away from the town where she was bullied by a red-faced boy and even the geraniums wilted in their pots. In the countryside with her grandmother, among the birds in the woods, herding

*her gentle cow, Sylvia was happy. When the hunter encountered her
in the forest and asked where he could find the white heron he wanted
so badly for his ornithology collection, she knew, instinctually, intu-
itively, that she would be selling her soul if she told this handsome
stranger, this Prince Charming, the way to the nest. Although it hurt
her to disappoint him, and her grandmother needed the money the
stranger offered for the rare bird's location, Sylvia refused to tell. She
chose instead to save the white heron, and herself.*

Tessa was one of the quiet students in my class, never
making a comment or asking a question. She sat among the
others, her long hair in a simple ponytail, her face free of makeup, listening and taking notes. I wouldn't remember her today if
it weren't for what happened on the final day of class, when the
exams had been handed in, and all the students except her had
filed out of the classroom for the last time.

She stood before me, having just placed on my desk her
examination blue book filled with handwritten answers. She
wore a raincoat, necessary in Seattle's damp climate where protection from rain and drizzle was always a practical idea. In her
left hand she held a gift bag, bright yellow, which she gave me
with a shy smile. "I know you don't read sci-fi," she said. "But I
think you might like these books—they're my favorites."

I took the paper bag containing the two hardbacks from
her with surprise, vaguely remembering that I'd announced
weeks ago that I didn't like science fiction, and promised to
read them.

But she wasn't done yet. "I want to thank you for this class."

*Her name was Minnie, a name that evokes the miniature, as in
small, reduced, scaled-down. Her maiden name was Foster, evoking
nurture and care, as in to foster a child. Her married name was
Wright, as in right versus wrong, implacable rigidity, the iron arm of
the law. Minnie's husband, older than she, a loner inured to the hardship
of homesteading, was cold and cruel to his young bride. With him*

Minnie withered, she failed to thrive, her personality wilted and her singing ceased. He was killing her as surely as if he had his hands around her neck. After decades of marriage, in the lonely hollow where the solitary farmhouse stood, among the windswept meadows, with no telephone or children or friends, Minnie snapped. John Wright broke her canary's neck one dark night; Minnie strangled her husband while he slept.

Standing in front of me in her navy raincoat, Tessa told me her story. She'd been living with her boyfriend and his mother in the mother's apartment. She didn't quite know how, but she found herself the only one in that small household going to college full time, working for a salary outside of school, and doing the cooking and cleaning in the apartment. This boyfriend didn't have a job or go to school, and neither did his mother. Yet Tessa did all the housework as a matter of course, with no one thinking it out of the ordinary.

The story of the young farm wife whose name was Minnie is not only about the death of a cruel husband, it is also about the mutinous sisterhood of the two women at the dead man's house, in Minnie's untidy kitchen, when they decided to protect their neighbor who should also have been their friend. They became a true jury of her peers, together saving Minnie from execution for what they saw as self-defense. In silent agreement, communicating exclusively with looks and gestures as they stood among the various men of the law, they kept secret the damning clues they'd found among the "trifles" that make up domestic space.

As Tessa spoke, I imagined her in the rain, trudging from bus stop to school to bus stop to work, hood up, head down, heavy book bag weighing on her shoulder. After a full day of classes and a shift at her job, she trudges up the dark stairs to the apartment with a bag of groceries weighing her down even further. Putting the key in the lock, she has to let herself in, as no one ever jumps to welcome her, to give her a kiss hello, to take her school bag off her shoulder and the groceries from her arms. Instead she is greeted with a boyfriend lounging on the sectional couch, TV on for the sixth, seventh, eighth hour, empty beer cans and cigarette butts on the sticky coffee table in front of him. The mother is in her own room, lying on the unmade bed and talking on the phone perhaps, or in her bathrobe next to her son, possibly smoking a cigarette herself. My imagination watched this mother let the ash collect until finally she flicks it off, sometimes aiming for the ashtray, sometimes not. It's always up to Tessa, to this student of mine, to put away the groceries, to prepare a meal for three, to clean the kitchen, to tidy the living room, to at last, around midnight or in the wee hours of the morning, open her books and do her schoolwork, schoolwork that includes reading stories for my class and writing essays about redefined quests and archetypes, heroic rebellions against patriarchal power, girls and women reclaiming their values and their lives.

Her name was Cleófilas and she left her six brothers who loved her and her widowed father who said "I will never abandon you" to marry the Prince Charming who lived across the border. There, in Texas, in the land of the American Dream, she found herself scared and abused, her only friends two neighbors whose names were Dolores and Soledad. One spring morning, Cleófilas sat with her toddler in the backyard across the river they called La Llorona. Feeling the pull of Llorona's legendary madness, Cleófilas decided to get help. Her story ends as she escapes from her violent husband and crosses back over the river with the aid of a woman whose name is Felicia. In her version of happily-ever-after, Cleófilas returns to her home, to her culture, to her family and friends.

That gray, damp Seattle day in the classroom after the final exam, Tessa stood before me after handing over the gift of two of her favorite books in their bright yellow bag. "Because of this class," she continued, "I realized how unfair it was for me to have to do all the work at home while I was the only one with a job and school."

Portrait of a Feminist

Her name was Janie. Janie rejected the control her first two hus-
bands tried to exert over her. One forced her to work hours in the fields,
plowing and digging and harvesting, or, when not outside, to clean the
farmhouse and cook the food. The other tried to "own" her as his trophy,
the young, pretty wife, by keeping her on a pedestal, in a gilded cage, to be
envied or coveted by the community but never—whether by playing chess
or exchanging gossip or telling jokes and tall tales—part of it. With the
third man, her true love, Janie insisted on what she wanted: working side
by side in the fields during the day, laughing and singing together in the
evenings, surrounding themselves always with friends and music and
merriment.

"Because of this class," said Tessa, still standing before me
in the emptied classroom, still in her raincoat, carrying only her
backpack now, her thoughtful gift having been transferred earlier to my gratified hand, "I realized I didn't want to keep being
used. It was wrong. I don't deserve that kind of treatment from
anyone. So I've broken up with my boyfriend and moved out."

I don't know how I reacted when I first heard this surprise
ending to Tessa's story, a story I never knew existed until
those few minutes at the end of the quarter, just the two of us in
the classroom surrounded by abandoned desks and chairs, the
exam instructions chalked on the board still to be erased. It's
probable that I tempered my feminist impulse to celebrate with
claps and cheers and maybe even high-fives, and instead merely
smiled a pleased smile and said I was glad the class helped. But
I do know that since then I've kept the memory of this moment
in the classroom with my student—of the story she told me
about her low self-esteem, about her mistreatment at the hands
of her boyfriend and his mother, about seeing herself in the
girls and women whose names were Sylvia and Minnie and
Cleófilas and Janie—close to me ever since.

Mujeriego

(Peru, 2000/2019)

*W*henever I think about Juan Luis, I think about his two wives—*sus dos mujeres*—and I'm reminded of telenovelas. My cousin's life played out for the extended family like those soap operas particular to Central and South American countries: clichéd stories of high drama and extreme passion told in a matter of months rather than the years of a *Days of Our Lives* or an *All My Children*. Juan Luis had a high school sweetheart, Adriana, on whom he cheated with Elena, a beauty pageant queen who worked as a secretary for his uncle. The stunning Elena, we all agreed, was the true love of his life—*su gran amor*. When I was young I accepted this explanation as gospel. It wasn't Juan Luis's fault he met Elena too late, after he'd committed to Adriana.

These days I understand this as a rationalization that allowed the rest of us to view him as a victim rather than a womanizer. He saw both Adriana and Elena until Adriana got pregnant. Rumor had it that Adriana got pregnant on purpose in order to force Juan Luis, her tall, handsome, basketball star boyfriend, to marry her. Only now, forty years later, do I question the stereotype that condemns the woman as manipulative and deceitful while absolving the man of any responsibility.

Why was this narrative of "one true love" so compelling? Why did I believe the skirting rationalizations, the defensive deceits? It was the glamor, the allure and mystique that surrounded Juan Luis. When we visited Lima in the years before he married, his bedroom was the farthest down the hall, a closed door, a dark mystery. Once I saw him mid-morning when we — my mother, sister, brother, and I — had already breakfasted with my aunt and uncle. Returning to our bedroom, I glimpsed my older cousin getting up from his bed — a wide mattress low to the ground with a single rumpled sheet for the hot summer nights — wearing only boxers, his tanned chest dark with curly black hair. His bedroom was wallpapered in a leopard pattern, the floor a golden shag. This scene I would think of later as part Yves Saint Laurent, part Halston.

Juan Luis is an alpha male, but a quiet one; he doesn't preen and pose, or flaunt a crude machismo. Instead, he is subtler, embodying an authority that people accept without question. On vacations in Peru when I was growing up, I watched it in action: if someone needed a ride, he'd take care of it; if my grandmother was anxious, he'd wrap his arms around her and make her laugh; if his parents needed a plumber, he'd send one to their place with his chauffeur. He drove long distances to settle business deals for his father while also making money himself to support his family. He was confident and self-possessed anywhere. On a morning of errands in a poor neighborhood, I sat in the backseat and watched as, prior to leaving the parked car for a few minutes, he reached under his seat and drew out a large silver pistol. I could tell it was heavy by the way his teenage son's hand dropped a bit as he accepted the gun from his father, who exited the car after instructing, *Keep this with you in case of any trouble.* To this day, Juan Luis takes charge of situations, fixes problems, conducts business, travels to Europe, commands a room. He's like a benevolent mafia don, a sort of good-looking Godfather.

His allure followed him into the early days of his first

marriage. As part of their honeymoon trip, Juan Luis and Adriana visited my family in Quito. I was an awkward twelve-year-old awed by Adriana's polished mannerisms, her filmy baby-doll nightgown, her long red nails and dramatic Diana Ross hair worn long and loose and brushed back from her face. All this softened into insignificance a slightly square jaw, a faintly bulbous nose. Self-assured and sexy, she, together with Juan Luis, embodied a thrilling glamor. She left a little bit of this glamor behind when she gave me her baby-doll nightgown before they flew to their next destination. She must have noticed I lusted after the clothes and jewelry, even the eyeshadow and lipstick that signaled her style, because I would follow her around, staring. I watched as she conversed with my mother, as she fingered her gold necklace, as she swept her hair back from her forehead with a practiced hand, and even as she ate. I wanted always to be in her presence, desperate to absorb everything I could of the sophistication she and Juan Luis took with them wherever they went.

Their joint mystique, however, was short-lived. Soon after returning to Lima, Juan Luis established a second home with Elena—his other woman, his girlfriend on the side, the one with a small nose and refined jawline, with full lips always ready to part in a soft smile. He worked hard to convince Elena that she was his priority, that he would divorce Adriana and marry her. Part of the story handed down to me as proof of true love, of a fairy tale romance, of his *gran amor* is that, in a dramatic gesture, Juan Luis flew to Italy, where Elena had moved to get away from him and his new wife after the wedding, and there used all of his powers—his charm and his humor, his looks and his natural magnetism—to woo her back with assurances of his undying passion. It worked.

Eventually Adriana found out about Elena, and the other house, and the subsequent second family. She fought to keep

Juan Luis by her side while ridding their lives of Elena, but failed. Despite bitter confrontations, blood-drawing scratches, vase-shattering fights, tearful calls to her in-laws begging for support, threats and ultimatums, Juan Luis never budged. He lied to her, soothed her, bribed her with jewelry and exotic vacations, but never wavered. He was faithful to his chosen lifestyle, living like a playboy in the seventies when some considered such a lifestyle fashionable, even enviable.

Some years later, after the questionable marriage license obtained in Panama with Elena and after the overdue divorce from Adriana, Juan Luis met a stewardess, willing and adventurous, on one of his many business flights to Buenos Aires. This stewardess knew from the beginning that he could not commit to her. Over forty, she asked him to give her a child. At least that's how my aunt quotes her whenever she tells the story. *"Dame un hijo."* And he obliged. Juan Luis then had three separate families with six children. Today, these six children know each other and love and support one another. There seems to be none of their mothers' resentment between them. I think about how younger generations can improve on older ones, how they can behave better. These children refuse a legacy of jealous feuding.

Decades ago, when the acrimony and competition remained solely between Adriana and Elena, my grandmother felt guilty. *"Creo que tal vez es mi culpa,"* she'd tell me over and over again, thinking it was her fault. "If I hadn't bought Juan Luis and Adriana the furniture set," she fretted, "maybe they wouldn't have felt obligated to marry. He could have married Elena from the beginning, *como debió de primera vez."*

I guess no one told her, fearing her staunch Catholicism, that it wasn't a furniture set that was the problem, it was a pregnancy.

As a child, I heard about these amorous adventures

through my mother, who heard it from her sister Clara, Juan Luis's mother and my mother's lifeline to her family in Peru. Although it was clear I was meant to side with my family and cousin, with my flesh and blood, there was always a little voice in me that tried to speak up for Adriana and later for Elena, for the women who were lied to and used as pawns in Juan Luis's creation of his ideal life. I grew up on telenovelas, first the ones we watched during the four years my family lived in Ecuador and then, back in the States, the ones offered on Univision and Telemundo. My mother and siblings and I looked forward to these yearlong sagas from Argentina and Mexico, Venezuela and Brazil, with names like *Cristal, Maria Celeste, Topacio,* and *Isaura*. Because I didn't question the fairy-tale narratives of these telenovelas, or the ideal femininity of the heroines they were named after, as a child I found the subplots of my extended Peruvian family to be more dramatic than disturbing. Always, however—even in the face of the excuses of my mother and aunt and grandmother for Juan Luis, and in spite of their automatic justifications for his behavior—part of me protested the acceptance of this casual chauvinism, recoiling from the injustice meted out to the real-life women in my family by a seductive, patronizing male.

Telenovela heroines of the seventies and eighties always and necessarily behaved properly; they were sweet and pretty and pure. As in the Gothic novels that reflected the sexual mores of nineteenth-century England, faithfulness and monogamy were essential to a woman's worth in the marriage market and the game of life. But what happens when Prince Charming refuses to live by the corresponding code of chivalry? What can women do when they uphold their side of the bargain only to find that their knight refuses to perform his honor-bound duty?

My cousin was so full of charisma, so funny, that he lit up a room just by walking into it. There was no resisting that kind of warmth and charm and ease. I was torn between worshiping him and judging him at a time when my own values, tentative and fragile, were just beginning to form.

*Y*ears afterward, when I'd been married almost eight years, we visited my relatives in Peru. As my husband and I rode in the car Juan Luis drove home from a restaurant in Lima, the three of us discussed the differences between Adriana and Elena (no one mentioned the stewardess). Adriana, Juan Luis explained to us, was a good mother, *una buena madre*. She was brainy, *inteligente*. But Elena, he said, who was not so intellectual, not so smart, was easy to be with. She was warm and welcoming. She knew how to make a home, *un hogar*.

I sat in the back seat and pondered this. Older by then, I knew that I believed my cousin's behavior reprehensible. But still, my emotions and my upbringing could manifest as insecurity, and there was always a rift between thought and feeling. So that night, even as I participated in the conversation, which was at once off-putting and totally familiar, I felt uncomfortable because of more than my cousin's chauvinism; some of my discomfort stemmed from a suspicion that I resembled Adriana more than I did Elena.

Adriana ended up teaching linguistics in college. She is completely bilingual in Spanish and English; in either language, her pronunciation is always precise, always perfect. With age, however, Adriana grew not just plumper but also, at least in accordance to Peru's strict standards, dumpier. "*Ay, que pena,*" my aunt used to say. "*Como se ha dejado la Adriana. Ya no se arregla bonito. ¡Y se ha puesto gordísima!*"

Adriana's face filled out and she now wears her kinky hair mannishly short. Her nails are no longer long and red but blunt and plain. Elena, on the other hand, still can't speak English but continues to fulfill the expectations of a specific set of beauty ideals. Fashionably thin, with smooth waves framing her face, she keeps her nails polished and manicured, her hair shiny and dyed, her body flexible and attractive with diet and exercise. She embodies a perfect woman to many in Peru as wife, mother, and homemaker. Unlike Adriana, who can be challenging, she is soft-spoken and good-humored. About her, my aunt says, *"Qué fina, qué linda es la Elena."*

In contrast, Adriana is ambitious. Not only does she work, she has a career. She doesn't feel it is her life's mission to maintain an exemplary home for her husband, to be an angel of the hearth. These comparisons prompted me that night to ask myself, what kind of wife was I? I hate cooking, cleaning, ironing. I love my reading, my studying—the scholarly life. Would I end up too smart, too hard, too mannish to keep my husband?

These are the kinds of questions that can haunt someone like me, brought up between cultures and value systems, between different ideals of femininity.

Now that he is getting older, it seems that Juan Luis wants his children, all of them, to be known. When I visited Lima last, almost two years ago, he mentioned over lunch that he has a son I'd never met. He also glossed over the fact that I'd never heard of this teenage relative of mine. I responded with surprise, but hid my dismay by asking him how many more children were going to come out of the woodwork. He laughed, but answered my questions with a seriousness that belied his initial casualness. This boy was a product of a relationship with a well-known television actress who wanted a child, but not a serious relationship. His situation suited her perfectly—they could have passion and a child together, but the public would never know. Juan Luis and his role in her life were kept hidden.

The boy was seventeen, and had already been introduced to his brothers and sisters. Apparently it was important to Juan Luis that his children all know each other and, I assume, love each other. But why at this particular moment in time? Perhaps Juan Luis felt his coming mortality. He was in his late sixties, his oldest child was in his early forties. As a father, he must have wanted his children to have each other for support into the future, after he was gone. My aunt and uncle, his parents, didn't know of this seventh child, of their grandson; his father had long ago made it clear that he wouldn't acknowledge any child after Elena's two sons. He'd lived through the drama of Adriana and Elena, and that was as far as he was prepared to go in condoning, even indirectly, his eldest son's womanizing.

As Juan Luis talked, prompted now and again by my questions, we both ate the ceviche and ají de gallina served on the house by his brother, who owns this waterfront restaurant in Lima's resort club on the coast. Juan Luis and I had found ourselves at the end of the long table filled with family, and thus able to have a relatively private conversation. As I listened to him, I looked through the floor-to-ceiling windows that lined two sides of the restaurant. I could see the stone promontory, a far less impressive version of the Cobb in Lyme Regis (memorialized forever in my mind by Jane Austen), on which people could stroll out toward the horizon and look back at the club on the shoreline. Seagulls flapped to and fro in their constant search for food, occasionally upstaged by a group of stately pelicans.

When I was a young child, around five and six and seven years old, I used to play with my siblings and cousins on the very beach fronting those windows. I didn't notice the birds then or think about the way a giant cross loomed over us from a hill at the end of the coastline. What we were always on the lookout for as children were the jellyfish that sometimes floated back and forth with the waves. Scared of their sting, we yelled warnings to each other if we spotted an *aguamala*, then went running back to safety on the sand. It was always hot, the air smelling faintly of brine, the sand warm under our feet. Those were long, lazy days, filled with beaches and pools, swimming and eating, Sunday luncheons at *la casa de las tías* (the three spinster aunties), driving around on errands, watching TV. But whatever we did on those vacations in Lima, we did it with family. I wondered if that was what Juan Luis wanted for his children and their children. Not playing on a beach, necessarily, or shrieking at the sight of an *aguamala*, but the constant connection, the togetherness, the feeling of belonging to a loving family.

As a child I thought of course women would do anything to be with Juan Luis, my cousin who was so handsome, so strong, so funny and charming and kind. A man who bothered—even at twenty and thirty and forty, even when he'd been at the beach all day or was on his way, freshly showered and cologned, to a nightclub or a party—to stop and talk and joke with his grandmother, an old lady with a silvery bun and a bottomless need for attention. An eldest brother and cousin who poked affectionate fun at the children and took us on occasion to get ice cream at the small bodega down the road from our gated community. A man who was an idol, a star; anyone would want to feel favored by him, even if for a moment.

Then, as an adult, one who took personally the suffering of women at the hands of men, I felt torn between my loyalty to Adriana and Elena and even the stewardess as women I saw victimized by Juan Luis's selfishness, and my loyalty to the cousin I'd grown up idolizing. Part of this was my unacknowledged gratitude for his attention, my own pleasure in his occasional notice of me. Juan Luis was the actor, the agent, bright and dominant, a person impossible to ignore. Who would even want to? The women, in contrast, seemed to me mere reflections, relatively insipid—not exactly boring, but not captivating in the way Juan Luis was.

And then I think about him now, now that I'm older and a mother, and I think of him differently. Does it count, somehow, that he was frequently left alone as a child? Should I factor in the way his parents fought a fight—all-encompassing, tumultuous, fierce—to find a loving space in which both of them could flourish? Their first years of parenthood were marked by a passionate engagement with each other, trying to negotiate a viable relationship for them both, one an entitled young man, rich and opinionated, and the other a seventeen-year-old girl pulled out of school, innocent and in love, a mother by eighteen. Juan Luis, born to these young inexperienced parents, was left by the wayside, so to speak, when his mother took a horse from their hacienda and galloped away from an argument with his father, which led to panicked phone calls and frantic searches. Juan Luis was again left by the wayside when his parents left him in Peru for almost a year, entrusted to the care of his grandmother while they lived in North Carolina, where his father finished his master's degree.

His parents went on to have three more children in rapid succession, then after a break of several years, another three, again in rapid succession. Where did this leave the young Juan Luis, the skinny wide-eyed boy, so quiet as he watched from the sidelines, a child cast as a supporting actor in the drama of his family?

When I think about Juan Luis's story now, I also think about his childhood neglect, and I wonder if womanizing was the way he found to get attention, to experience intense and focused love and admiration—feelings that as a child he missed, perhaps, from his mother and father.

Sons

(California, 1991)

When I was young, I planned on having girls. My imagined readers as I wrote in my diary were my future daughters. We would be a mini-tribe of Amazons, strong and powerful and knowledgeable. Together, we would be versed in different cultures and subcultures that pressure us as women to be *Other*, other than ourselves, other than the Self, objects rather than Subjects with a capital S. I would teach them—as a role model, in real time, as well as through the words in my diary. My daughters would grow up empowered by knowledge: the "large" knowledge of the world and how it works, as well as the "small" knowledge of my past, my experiences, my errors and blunders. They would learn and benefit, avoiding their mother's mistakes and becoming stronger for it. It gave me satisfaction to write for these girl babies as yet unconceived. I would imagine my daughters reading the words, seeing the images, envisioning the experiences, and then being motivated to read on, to desire the details of a flirtation, a dangerous moment skirted, an embarrassment they could sidestep. My diary had a purpose, and I found myself shaping what I wrote for a specific set of female eyes.

Then I had two boys.

Self and Mother

(Seattle, 1999)

I walked one day after lunch in the high school cafeteria to the lockers with my best friend. International like me, she had lived in different countries, and traveled around the world with her family. She was telling me about her claustrophobia on planes, how she felt trapped in a tiny capsule thousands of feet above the air.

"I just can't stop thinking about how I can't get out. No matter what."

That was it. Just sixteen and highly suggestible, I caught her phobia and had trouble flying from that point forward. As the plane took off, I panicked, my breath becoming shallow, my heart beating uncontrollably, my knuckles white as I alternately gripped the armrests and pinched my skin on my arm, frantic for distraction. I imagined having a breakdown, running up and down the aisles, making a scene. Of course I never did, but the fear that I might made me dread flying.

I found that this phobia only abated after my son was born. One of the first times I flew with him, I did so without taking the drugs that helped with my anxiety because I didn't want to taint the breast milk that was then his only sustenance. My stomach lurched when I first saw on the tarmac the small plane that was going to take us from Seattle to Portland on our way to San Francisco. So compact it seated just twenty passengers, its ceiling prevented me from standing upright as I negotiated the aisle carrying my son, the diaper bag, and the car seat. But what I noticed as we took off was a tempering, a softening of my fear. There were twinges of the old nerves, but not the sharp stabs of panic. I was less afraid, less worried about my person, because I was with my son. It seems that because I had to take care of him, I put my fears for myself aside. He came first.

That afternoon when my son was only a few months old and I stepped into the plane I feared would trigger my claustrophobia, something shifted for me. Although I didn't know it at the time—I was too busy with the daily demands of caring for an infant—something inside me had changed: what was before abstract and theoretical, my sense of duty and even my survival instincts, had distilled to an essence that was different from what was before.

I didn't foresee this shift; how could I? For me it was a part of maturing, of the growth that comes with time and experience.

For most of my conscious life, my fearful nature, my innate tendency toward safety and caution, had manifested in a need for control. Control meant answers—concrete, complete, whole, and irrevocable. Never had I had a tolerance for ambiguity, or the capacity to think in Venn diagrams in order to center what overlaps. Unlike Fa Mu Lan, Maxine Hong Kingston's woman warrior, I could not open my mind wide enough to hold paradoxes; instead I wanted to fight the known, well-defined, never-changing enemy. But at that time in my life—and, ironically, in the claustrophobic space of a small plane—my core values, my defining principles, including a hard and immature feminism, were both complicated and refined by the unconditional love of mother for child.

Two, maybe three years into my relationship with my husband, when we were still boyfriend and girlfriend, still "dating," we sat in my car before having lunch at a restaurant in Palo Alto. I sat in the driver's seat and my boyfriend in the passenger seat next to me as we discussed my future career. His had been settled almost two decades earlier, decided by him in his seventh year of life: he was going to be a doctor (and, indeed, on this day it was between medical school classes that he was meeting me for lunch).

I remember we both liked the idea of English as a major for me because teaching would leave me free during winter holidays and summer vacations to raise a family. I was thinking ahead to a time when I could have both career and family, when I could "have it all," work satisfaction and maternal fulfillment. Did I think then that I was sacrificing something with my plans? That my career would take a backseat to my husband's so I could satisfy my instincts to nurture my children beyond breastfeeding?

I feel sad, and like a traitor, just thinking about my beloved feminism as "hard" and "immature." But with the benefit of hindsight, that's what it was. It was a feminism first internalized then lived in rigid binaries: those old clichés, black and white, hot and cold, dark and light . . . For most of my life I under-stood feminism as both weapon and cause in a fight for justice. The good guys (gals?—even our speech betrays us) were clearly feminist women, the bad side equally obvious: patriarchal culture, patriarchal men.

Always, however, at least in the back of my mind, sat the knowledge that I lacked true options, that I wasn't free to choose my future because I was a woman. My choices and my decisions would always be mediated by my sex and gender. I ended up choosing motherhood in a marriage to a man who could make enough money to support us all rather than fighting to nurture my career. I sensed then, intuited at some level, what is so clear to me now in middle age: my gendered life set up motherhood and feminism in competition, a boxing match or a race. And that tension calmed only with actual motherhood.

It's as if my core self (for most of my life saturated by feminism) and my maternal identity (mother of two boys) were two race horses on the track—ears back and eyes wide, necks straining and legs pumping—and what I did *not* anticipate as a younger woman looking into the future happened. Maternal Identity, who lagged behind for the first third of the race, quite suddenly leapt forward. There was no sense of strain; there was no frothing sweat. Instead there was an ease, and Maternal Identity looked almost balletic as she caught up with Feminist Self. And there the two have remained, no longer competing, instead cantering side by side. It is no longer a race.

Among all the memories and images of that day—the packing, the breastfeeding, the constant concerns about the baby, the shock at the size of the plane, the hunching over to get to my seat—there is one that stands out. I assume that because our plane was so small we flew lower than regular jetliners. I remember at one point looking out the window and seeing Mount St. Helens. We were so close to the huge volcano, I felt as if I could reach out and touch the pure, powdery snow with my fingertips. Just a short year before, preoccupied with self-distraction, with pulling down the blind, reading a book, trying to ignore the fact that I was on a plane, I would have missed this sight—stunning, awesome, transcendent—completely.

The Sandal

(Seattle, 1999)

I drive in the late-night dark to the emergency room with my mother. I've never been there before; it's just a clinic, but close by and open all night. I left my husband at home, sound asleep, after I lifted the baby from his usual position snuggled in bed next to us to buckle him, still sleeping, into his car seat.

My mother, visiting Seattle from California, had been helping in the garden. A hands-on kind of mother, she'd decided earlier today to tackle the ivy. In the back, masses of thick leaves spread up and out between shrubs and trees. My mother hates ivy. Too big, too strong, too invasive. She was struggling with the tangled vines in rubber flip flops, exposed feet wading in the undergrowth, when she felt the bite. Together we examined the foot and determined that it must have been a spider. Then, within the hour, the foot swelled, engorging to double its usual size. Images of deadly venom, of blood infection, of red streaks making their way up to the heart, came to mind. I made an executive decision: we must see a doctor, just in case. My mother has always taken care of me; all my life she's worried about me, defended me, protected me. Now it's my turn.

As we drive sitting companionably in the heated warmth of the car's interior, it seems as if everyone else in the quiet suburb sleeps cocooned in houses behind closed curtains and lowered shades, a sensation that makes our journey feel mystical, as if we are the only people alive, the car a kind of spaceship exploring uninhabited territory. Pine trees and hedges pass by in the silent night. This landscape, coupled with consistently gray skies, can feel oppressive, almost claustrophobic. Tonight the sky, overcast all day, has darkened impenetrably, and the headlights alone brighten the road.

Then—so suddenly that I slam on the brakes—there's a bundle in the middle of the road. What is it? A garbage bag? A discarded piece of clothing? Or—for one horrifying instant—an infant in a blanket?

But no, squinting into the high beams' path, I can tell it's a cat lying on its side. Very weak, it lifts its head to confront this latest threat—the car with its thrumming engine and blinding lights. It's been hit and left on the road in the darkness. I'm not sure what to do. I imagine another car driving by that can't stop in time, another driver, distracted by radio dials or sleepiness, who doesn't see the cat before it's too late. I pull over to the side of the street.

After putting the car in park and leaving the engine running to keep the heater on for my mother and son, I walk toward the injured animal, trying to soothe it from a distance by murmuring, *It's okay . . . It'll be okay*, almost as if it were a child in distress. But the cat, feral with pain, lifts its head again and hisses, fur electrified, fangs exposed. I return to the car, stressing about my baby in the back, trustfully asleep, my mother in the passenger seat, possibly with blood poisoning, and now this cat in front of us, suffering.

Feeling helpless, I guide the car on the shoulder of the road. With careful maneuvering, I give the wounded cat a wide berth, finally leaving it behind in the wake of our darkness as we continue to the twenty-four-hour fluorescence of the emergency room.

Portrait of a Feminist

*T*his moment in the dark, saturated, it seems to me, by
vulnerability—baby, mother, cat—takes me back three
years to Boston in the summer. It's the Fourth of July and
people stroll in the balmy evening on their way to and from
restaurants and bars and ice cream parlors. The atmosphere is
festive, relaxed. On the sidewalk, my husband and I uninten-
tionally catch up to a family, an All-American family, heading
in the same direction. There is the father: blond, tall, barrel-
chested, wearing a Hawaiian vacation shirt and pale linen
slacks. There is the wife: blonde and petite and delicately
boned, wearing a flowery skirt and kitten-heeled slingbacks.
There is the daughter: about eleven. A gangly, gawky eleven.
Long, skinny legs and knobby knees, cotton dress and summer
cardigan, sandals.

I take this in as we follow the family, as around us each
couple or group in the crowd forms their own circle of intimate
interaction. When we get nearer to them, I see the father grab
the daughter by the neck, a neck that looks tender and pale,
exposed as it is between two blonde braids, and throw her
against the brick wall of an adjacent building. I see the meaty
hand encircling the slim young neck, a neck caught off guard,
and the daughter's reaction—startled, dismayed, scared. Her
head bounces against the brick. The father presses the daughter
up until she dangles from his hold while she clutches convul-
sively at his arm. I hear the mother pleading in a soft, high
voice, "David! Stop . . . David!"

But I am the one who stops—to watch, to witness. I am
desperate to save the girl. This father, this man, is like a figure
in a Stephen King story, in a horror movie. The kind where the
safe, conventional figure transforms, flesh and bones morphing

into a monster, a brute, a beast. The girl, the victim, humiliated and shamed and frightened, never has a chance.

My husband senses my desperation. "Let's go," he says, "We can't do anything about it. He might beat *us* up."

I recognize that he's right, that we can't act without jeopardizing ourselves. This is before cell phones; we can't take a video as evidence or dial 911 and, as with magical lamps that conjure genies to do one's bidding, summon the police out of thin air.

I wish for superhero powers; I want bionic arms that can rescue, an invincible body that can protect. I wish with desperation that I had the strength to lift this bully by *his* neck and toss him aside. Instead, I can only refuse to leave before the scene somehow resolves itself, hovering at the periphery and wishing to do something, to say something, but powerless to act.

When the father finally lets go, the daughter falls to the ground. As she rights herself, trembling, her mother picks up the sandal that had loosened with the impact of the girl's body against the wall and tumbled off. Quickly, like a nervous bird, she puts it back on her daughter's foot. Then the family continues to walk toward their destination, blending into the weekend crowds as if nothing untoward has happened. But before they disappear, I notice the father's hand placed once again on the daughter, who walks with shoulders hunched and head bowed, pressing heavily on her neck as he propels her forward—a weight, a warning, a guarantee of her continued submission.

*A*rriving at the clinic, I pull into the patient loading zone, the space closest to the sliding doors. I tell my mother I can't stop thinking about the cat.

"While you're seeing the doctor, why don't I go back and try to figure something out?" I suggest.

My mother, also concerned, agrees—*Okay, mi vida*. I watch as she hobbles through the glass doors when they open automatically for her, then wait until she returns to the entryway and gives me a thumbs up: yes, a doctor will see her, I can go now.

Back at the cat, I park again on the shoulder of the street, lights aimed at the dark mound to warn drivers as they travel down the road. It's in the pioneer days of cell phones, so I'm able to call 411 for the numbers of all the agencies I can think of that might be able to help. I try the Humane Society— closed. I try Wild Care—nothing. I try the local police—they tell me to call the Humane Society. I try the Humane Society again—still no answer. Frustrated, I try the police station once more. This time I detail the plight of the cat, who hisses and snarls when approached, and my plight as a witness who wants to prevent further injury but doesn't know how. When the police agree to come, I lean back in my seat reassured, my baby still asleep in the back, high beams cutting through the darkness, staring at the cat. Several cars come by and my plan works: the lights alert them to slow down and they cautiously drive past us.

When the two policemen arrive, I greet them with relief. I watch as they open the trunk of their vehicle, where they've stashed thick gloves and a container. Together they walk to the cat. The one with the gloves gently picks it up as the other positions the cage. I'm comforted myself when I hear them say, "Hey there, buddy . . . Don't worry, we got you."

After settling the container carefully in the backseat of the police car, they come to my window to thank me for my efforts.

"Thank *you*," is all I can think to reply, their gratitude taking me off guard. To me, they are the rescuers, the saviors, the guardians—big, burly angels wearing uniforms. I know that without them I would have been destined for weeks if not months and years to relive my failure, once again, to intervene.

With the burden of responsibility lifted, I make a U-turn toward the clinic, where my mother waits for me. When I get there, she will tell me the good news that her foot will be fine and I will relate the saga of the cat rescue. Then, with the baby still asleep in the backseat, we will drive together to the safety of the house with its warm rooms and soft beds, threat and danger retreating with the lightening sky.

Regrets

(California/Seattle/Italy, 1984–2000)

*J*ust the other day, at the age of fifty-six, I noticed for the first time that the word *regret* shares five of its first six letters with the Spanish word *regresar*. *Regret* is the sorrow aroused by circumstances beyond one's power to repair. *To regret* is to feel remorse for an act or fault. The verb root *re* signals the idea of "again" or "once more."

What fascinates me: *Regresar* means to go back, to return. Together, *regret* and *regresar* convey a yearning for a going-back, for another chance, a fresh start.

A caveat: This story is not about big regrets, those life-changing moments that cause deep wounds and enduring scars; it is instead about small regrets, about three moments in my life that are relatively insignificant, seemingly forgettable, but have stayed with me nonetheless, floating for some reason in the periphery of my mind, perhaps linked one with the other by context or age or developmental stage—it's hard to know exactly why we remember what we do, or why some memories always seem to bring up others.

What I do know: when I recall each of these moments, I wish I could go back. I want to return in order to change things. I want a redo.

*T*hat night, the club had shut down and it was just past two in the morning. Enika and I were warm and sweaty from the small, enclosed space where we'd spent the last few hours dancing to the latest imported music from England—Alphaville, Spandau Ballet, Thompson Twins, New Order.

As we walked toward my car I was on my guard, looking for a fight. Already annoyed, my irritation spiked when we drew near and I realized from the rumbling and shaking that the Plymouth Valiant's massive V8 engine was on. I peered into the window and saw our third friend, Daniel Jameson, lying on the backseat, curled up in a fetal position. Daniel's closed eyes, his child's pose, did nothing to calm me.

Earlier that evening: The three of us were in my car. I drove, Enika and Daniel sat next to me on the front seat, not one of us thought to wear a seatbelt. On the radio, Prince's "When Doves Cry" announced itself with the soft wail of the guitar and the sad lyrics about fathers who are too demanding, mothers who are never satisfied, the young couple who, perhaps inheriting these traits, can't seem to get along. Enika started to sing with the radio, Daniel harmonized, and I joined in for the chorus. The three of us were high on singing together, on the angst and disaffection the lyrics evoked, on leaving the suburbs for the city in search of adventure in San Francisco's small underground club scene.

Then the night took a turn. Even before we parked outside the club and exited the car. Perhaps merely minutes after combining our voices—Enika's good, Daniel's medium, mine bad—to sing along with Prince. Daniel had brought alcohol for himself. The underground clubs, pop-ups often in warehouses down dark alleys in industrial neighborhoods, didn't offer drinks of any kind. His drink of choice, the one he had that evening in the car, was rum and Coke. Had he premixed it? In a thermos of some kind? I don't recall. I was driving. He was drinking. We were singing. The Plymouth Valiant, the rum and Coke, the radio and the song. Daniel talked of a father—too cold? Contemptuous? Angry? Violent? I don't remember the particulars. Just his drinking, my driving, his voice more and more quiet, more and more sad. *Is this what it sounds like when doves cry?*

Poor Daniel, I think today, now that I'm older, over a quarter-century older, and a mother. *Daniel, tall and lanky and effeminate, with the five o'clock shadow he was forever shaving and the mole on his cheek he always penciled into a beauty mark before going out. Poor Daniel, disowned and disinherited, orphaned by paternal prejudice and fear, ignorance and disgust.* Back then, however, I did not—I could not—either understand or empathize.

In the club, among the shadowy figures and the dancing bodies, surrounded by the pulse of the music and the beat of the bass, Daniel leaned in close to my ear. "Can I have the keys to the car?"

What? Why? I was loath to relinquish these keys to anyone. The car represented freedom and mobility for me; it represented control over what we did, when we did it, how we did it. Giving the keys to Daniel—who, unlike Enika, was a secondary friend, not of the inner circle—felt inappropriate and strange. But he was sick; he had drunk too much too soon and too fast. His mood had shifted earlier, when still in the car, from exuberant to morose. So, knowing it was the right thing to do, I placed the keys in the palm of his outstretched hand and watched him, with his tall thin body, his colorful shirt and slim trousers, his slicked-back, dyed-blonde hair, disappear into the crowd on his way to the exit.

What happened after Enika and I got back to the car, after

we danced every song played, after the music went off and the lights went on? What happened after I peered into the window and saw Daniel curled up in the back, the car engine vibrating and the heater on high? These were the days, mind you, when I routinely checked in between the seats, in the glove compartment, on the floor, and under the mats for stray coins to use for gas, gas that was being wasted, or so I believed, every second the car's fuel-guzzling engine idled so that Daniel—a secondary friend, not of the inner circle—could stay warm in the cold San Francisco night.

If I could rewrite history—if, knowing and feeling what I know and feel now, I could go back in time and do it differently, this is what would happen:

I open the driver's door and prepare to enter with care so as not to wake Daniel, while at the same time gesturing to Enika with a finger to my lips and a nod toward the back where he lies curled on his side, hands between his knees. If he wakes even after I slip into the car, shutting the door with a soft click, and depress the gas pedal as slowly as possible to soften the roar of the engine, I inquire, right away, before any potential apologies or self-recrimination on his part, how he feels—is he okay, is he sick, is he sad? In this re-visioned moment of the past I am gentle, I am kind, I am patient and sympathetic and understanding. If he seems open to it, answering my questions readily, we talk about what made him feel bad, maybe drinking too quickly, maybe the drink itself, and about what made him feel sad, perhaps the memories of his father that triggered feelings of alienation and loneliness. Enika and I tell him how great he is, how fashionable and creative, how he is such a good dancer, a cool dresser, how his taste in music is impeccable. We make him feel appreciated. We build him up.

What actually happened:

I rapped on the back window with my knuckles, angry. Daniel woke with a start, confused. Enika and I got in the front of the car; I was silent and seething. Did Daniel apologize? Was he humble with regret at having put me out, at having wasted gas and money by leaving on the car, with its ridiculously powerful engine, so that he could blast the heater? Did he acknowledge the inconvenience on me, the owner of the car, the payer of the gas, the driver for the night's activities? I don't remember.

What I do remember: anger and contempt on my part, confusion and sadness on his.

What I feel now: regret.

Loren walked away and her back looked lonely. It looked like resignation, disappointment, even betrayal. It could have had something to do with a slight droop of the shoulders, a tilt of the head, even the exposed neck under a short haircut. As I watched, a hint of guilt—of not having gotten it right, of having miscommunicated and misunderstood—grew stronger inside me, a pang in my chest. Loren was walking away from me and Enika, two fellow students, two young women like herself whom she thought she could trust. I was her suitemate at the all-women's dorm on campus, and we shared—besides a living space—confidences, insecurities, and doubts as we navigated our huge public university.

What happened, what was said, right before Loren walked away, her back so lonely seeming? What did she and Enika and I talk about after running into each other at school, the hundreds of other students streaming past us on the crowded campus thoroughfare, during that busy time in between classes in the middle of a weekday?

The problem that started it all was a homework assignment for a gender studies course. We had to attend an event, a rally, a talk, anything having something to do with women and their rights. Enika and I chose a poetry reading the professor had helpfully included in a list of possibilities. An all-women poetry reading. A feminist poetry reading. Loren wanted to know how it had gone, whether it was terrible or scary or boring or—possibly—fun, inspiring, and communal.

If, again, I could go back in time, if I could rewrite history, if I were granted, somehow, a redo, this is how my side of the conversation would go:

At first I didn't know what to expect, but then it was pretty cool.
The women who read were really honest and emotional.
Everyone sat in a circle, and everyone was super welcoming.
The audience nodded during the readings and clapped afterward.
I don't even know why I was nervous in the first place.

What was actually said, or implied, or suggested, if not in word then in tone, gesture, and facial expression that may have triggered the walking away, the lonesome back:

It was really weird.

There was such a granola, hippie feeling.

There were so many dreadlocks.

There was that smell, patchouli or something?

There were lots of lesbians there.

Loren looked at us, from me to Enika to me again, and laughed. It was a nervous laugh, uneasy. She didn't join my disdain toward the scene at the poetry reading. Ending the conversation with a quick "See you later," she turned and walked away from us.

Enika didn't comment on Loren's reaction, at her affect as she heard me describe the poets and the reading and the Berkeley café venue, at her dejected air and lonely back. Enika and I had debriefed in full the night before, after we, having observed enough to write our assignment, left the reading early, hoping no one noticed our defection. She thought the way I did, at least she said so at the time. This was before she came out as gay. Before she discovered she was a lesbian. Before our endless discussions about her identity, her sexuality, her attraction to women rather than men.

Portrait of a Feminist

Some months later, Enika and Loren and I found ourselves together again. This time we were at a party, in a student's apartment near campus. There was a stereo with records playing, there was vodka, a stained couch, and cheap student lamps. The scuffed coffee table was crowded with matches, cigarette packs, full ashtrays, and open beer cans. There was also Ecstasy. A small blue pill, this drug was all the rage on campuses and in clubs. I'd never tried it. But Loren had just taken one. She told us about it, already moving around the living room seductively, her senses, especially touch, turned up high. She twirled toward the record player, and as she bent down to fiddle with the needle, she rubbed her backside against Enika's thigh.

Wow. I looked at Loren's backside, rubbing back and forth, I looked at Enika's face. Enika looked at me. This was new and unexpected. We would talk about this moment again and again in the days that followed. About what it meant. About Loren's feelings. Had she merely been taking advantage of the nearest thigh to maximize the tactile pleasure enhanced by the Ecstasy? Or was there a particular draw to Enika, a lesbian still in hiding, making itself known in this moment at an apartment party full of music and drinks and pills? Perhaps Loren was bisexual or gay. Perhaps she'd always sensed in Enika a sensuality open to women. Perhaps this was another overture, more obvious, more direct, than a feeling-out during a conversation in the middle of the day, in the middle of a crowded campus.

We will never know, because Enika, stepping back, moved away from Loren.

Was a missed opportunity the punishment for her non-response to Loren that night? If Enika could go through a portal back in time, back to the night of the party, would she jump at the chance to rewrite the narrative of what happened? Would she respond with enthusiasm instead of rejection and open herself to a sexual encounter, a possible relationship with another young woman, perhaps the first of its kind for Loren as well as for herself?

If so, what was my punishment for my narrow, fearful, closed-minded reaction to Loren's bid for connection, for understanding, that day on campus when we talked about women's poetry? It could be that it is regret. For letting my fear make me hard and dismissive. For letting my immaturity govern my words. For disappointing and alienating someone who didn't deserve it.

*W*earing my L.L. Bean version of the ubiquitous "barn coat" so popular in mid-nineties Seattle, I watched as if from afar. This is my memory, at least. That I was sitting distant from the object of my gaze, that I was at a table apart from hers in my graduate department's common room, protected by my boots and my jeans and my barn coat. Our shared space was itself alienating. Part of a cement-block building, this room was plain and angular, with some thin bookshelves, aluminum windows that looked out at the constant gray, metal heater vents lining the walls, a few tables with plastic chairs placed at random here and there. In reality, I probably sat at the same round conference table as the woman I was staring at; yet somehow, more fittingly, my memory has me sitting at another table, as if watching from the audience a tableaux: Mother with Baby, Madonna and Child.

The mother in this case was not quite a Madonna with her half-immortal Christ Child, but rather an ordinary student who happened to have had a baby during her tenure in graduate school. She was older than me, and a couple of years ahead in her studies. I believe we were in some kind of meeting, a meeting that necessitated us gathering together in the common room, around the same table. So I probably was sitting near her, perhaps even next to her, as she lifted her shirt and pulled down her bra to feed her infant.

What I wish happened next:

I smile as the baby snuffles and swallows. I admire my fellow student's ability to nurture her child while attending school, going to meetings, and collaborating with other students. I sympathize with any challenges she might have—the juggling of time, the demands of the body vs. the mind, housework vs. homework, domesticity and diapers and feedings versus research and writing and teaching. I ask, "How are you doing? Are you getting some sleep? How old is the baby? Can I hold her?" I root for my colleague's right to feed her infant wherever and whenever she needs to, without leaving the room for "privacy," without using a blanket or shawl to cover her chest as if shielding something shameful.

This is what actually happened:

The shirt went up and the bra went down. I saw a bare breast, an exposed nipple before the baby latched on. Past the baby's head, I could still see a patch of pale flesh. I stared in a kind of astonished outrage. We were sitting in the *common room.* In our *department's building.* At *school.* There were *male students* at the table with us. How could she be so calm? So unperturbed? So *unselfconscious*?

Some years later, just after defending my dissertation in the same concrete building that housed the inhospitable common room, I traveled to warm, sunny Italy with my family, my husband, and my seven-month-old baby. We were touring Florence's Uffizi Galleries, walking among the famous paintings, Botticelli's *Venus* being one of them, as well as several of the Madonna and Child, complete with exposed, lactating breasts. I took a break to sit on a bench in a corridor I remember as sunlit, lined here and there with lesser statues, many of which displayed not just naked breasts but also penises. My son was hungry and I had to feed him.

As I breastfed, a docent approached me, brow furrowed, lips pursed, finger pointed. In Italian, she told me I couldn't breastfeed in the museum. It wasn't allowed. I looked up at her from my seat on the bench, in a corridor connecting rooms filled with exposed chests and genitalia. With the Mother of God holding her child, nipples at the ready. In one, the infant Messiah grasped a breast with dimpled fingers while looking at the viewer as if in defiance.

What happened next:

Although confused by this contradiction, I acquiesced to the woman's wish that I stop breastfeeding, that I pull up my bra and pull down my shirt, that I cover my shameful, lactating body. I couldn't be bothered to argue in Italian, to point out the obvious ironies in this museum docent's demands that I cover my embarrassing, inappropriate breast.

What I wish I had said but didn't need to, because my sister said it for me:

"*Perché no?*" she asked of the scolding docent. "Why can't she breastfeed here?"

"It isn't appropriate," the docent answered. "It isn't proper. It isn't respectful. Would she breastfeed in an *American* museum? *Credo di no!*"

"But you're wrong," came back my sister. "She *would* breastfeed in a museum in America. She *does* breastfeed in public in America. She's not embarrassed by it—there's nothing to be embarrassed about!"

My sister was right. By that time, I had unlearned all my shame around breastfeeding in public. I found it a wonderful, miraculous tool in caring for my child. I could feed him anytime and anywhere! I had no need for bottles or formula or pumps; I had no need of sterilizing or heating or cooling. My body had it all. The food, the nutrition, the soothing. And I loved it. I loved breastfeeding in the morning and at night, when my baby first woke and before he fell asleep, in our family bed or on a museum bench.

My regret is that I didn't have this knowledge, this all-encompassing understanding of breastfeeding as natural and good, that day in the graduate school's common room, that day when I watched and judged. The day I wish I had—instead—admired and sympathized and encouraged.

*W*hat was wrong with me in those moments in high school and university and graduate school? Why was I so hard and rigid, so inflexible? I wonder now where my compassion was as a person and a feminist. Maybe I couldn't see vulnerability in Daniel because he was a man. Still in high school, with feminist discourse so new to me, it could be that I saw the world as divided into binaries: male/female, us against them, either/or. No humanism, no alternative reimagining of the world. Perhaps I couldn't see the ask in Loren's questions, the bid for connection in her expression, because I was scared of the alien, the unfamiliar, the *not-me*. It might be that I judged my colleague's public breastfeeding so severely because I had internalized my mother's prudishness—I never saw her breasts, I never saw her naked. She was private about her feminine body to the point of stealth and secrecy.

It could be that I regret the person I once was because I am no longer her. It also could be that this is inevitable: no one who remembers, who engages in the questioning, searching, probing act of remembering—unless they know of an actual portal to the past, that is—can escape this type of regret.

These questions and suppositions might explain my behavior in the earlier stages of my life. They might extend to my younger self what I couldn't extend to Daniel and Loren and the breastfeeding graduate student: some compassion, some understanding. They might give the young me a small break in this exercise in self-judgment and shame. Even so, they cannot erase my regret.

In the Palace Gardens

(Egypt, 2008)

I'm looking out of the large picture window from the seventh floor at the Sheraton Montazah Hotel in Alexandria. Still in their matching pajamas, my children play behind me on the bed with their toys from home and treasures purchased over the past few days at gift shops and museums. From a certain angle, I can see the gardens of King Farouk's summer palace across the street from the hotel, at the end of the western harbor, before you get to the famous corniche. Ornate with carved moldings and fanciful turrets, the palace has been situated to maximize views of the Mediterranean's pale sunrises and dramatic sunsets.

The previous day, on a visit to the palace's blue and gold dining room where we were served traditional afternoon tea in silver pots and delicate china, I'd seen in the garden a couple. They were a young couple, a romantic couple. Seated on one of the numerous benches among the tall palms, they appeared to be engaging in the age-old ritual of love and flirtation. The young man leaned toward the young woman. She bent her head, seemingly shy. He insisted. She smiled. He said something. She laughed. They held hands. Together, they'd created a small, private world into which no one else could enter.

I wonder, as I stand at the window, looking down toward the garden, about the couple's proximity to each other, for although they didn't kiss or caress, at times their heads almost met, and the way they positioned their bodies toward one another was intimate, yearning.

I wonder because the young woman was wearing hijab. In jeans and a fitted shirt with the requisite long sleeves, she wore a scarf fastened scrupulously under her chin and over a tight cap that securely hid her hairline, denying all access to ears, neck, or even wisps of hair. This type of hijab has often reminded me of a sister's habit—just the headdress, with its close-fitting coif and white wimple.

I wonder at the physicality this couple shared in public. How could they have been alone and unchaperoned, sometimes touching skin to skin, even if just that of their hands? I've always thought of the hijab as a kind of nun's veil, a signal that the flesh it shields is off-limits, untouchable outside the home and legitimized relationships like husband and wife or mother and son.

*I*n Lima there's an open space that is, like this palatial garden on the Mediterranean, adjacent to the ocean. Called El Parque del Amor, it is unique because of "El Beso," the large statue of two people, man and woman, in erotic, supine embrace. Couples gather there on warm evenings, on weekend afternoons, in the dark, enveloping night. They sit on the grass, sometimes after unfurling the blankets they've brought with them, talking and kissing, lying down to make out, look into each other's eyes, and caress each other's faces. There are parks all over the city devoted to this pastime, and no Limenean finds it remarkable or pauses to gaze at the dozens of couples decorating the gardens along with the ferns and acacia trees. It is a common spectacle, sanctioned and public. But what about here, in Egypt, in this coastal city with its domes and minarets, with its long history of Islamic faith and lifestyle? I don't know if it's just me who couldn't get past the nun-like hijab to focus instead on the girl's trendy jeans and colorful shirt, both of which speak to romance and youth rather than caution and chastity.

ater that morning, while my husband is at a conference, I leave the hotel and cross a busy street with my two sons, each of my hands holding tightly onto one of theirs. All the streets seem busy here, with cars and taxis and vans vying for space, crowding into three, sometimes four lanes where officially there are only two. There's the constant honking—automatic, almost unconscious—that helps drivers expertly avoid each other, often, it seems to me, by a hair's breadth. There are no crosswalks; I can never find a pedestrian right-of-way. Cars here do not, will not, pause for anyone.

When we make it to the other side, and are safe on a sidewalk lined with restaurants and cafés, a man passing calls out something rude. He, I know, is referring to my foreignness; he has caught me out, discovered me as Western, as Other. I realize I don't have the scarf I usually wear draped around my shoulders to cover the lower-cut shirts and blouses I favor. I've left my neck and the top of my chest bare and open to view. No cleavage, but enough skin to mark me as different, and immodest.

This small encounter leaves me shaken. I have on wide-legged pants, a scoop-necked T-shirt, and a denim blazer. Why should I be targeted? I realize I've grown comfortable with being mistaken for Egyptian, for being addressed in Arabic, for being the object of attention as the mother of two small boys in a city that loves children. I don't like this open disrespect, this righteous contempt of my clothing and my body, of me.

I n Lima when my mother came of age, there was a tradition of giving *piropos*. As far as I can make out, this tradition was ritualized flirtation, a choreographed dance of attraction and acknowledgement between youth on the cusp of maturity—those who are leaving the innocence of childhood behind but are not yet burdened by the responsibility of adulthood. Young men stood on street corners and at the edges of parks, or walked around a city square in groups, calling out to pretty young women gathered in pairs or groups of friends themselves. These *piropos* were often elaborate compliments, sometimes bordering on the poetic. Although this custom carried the taint of patriarchy, with men objectifying women with their appraising gaze, it still seems so civilized, so elegant, especially when viewed through the softening prism of nostalgia. I can see the boys in their pleated slacks and dark, precisely combed hair; I can see the girls in their cinched waists and full skirts, their hair styled and shaped into variations of the bouffant. One definition of a *piropo* is "an expression of gratitude for beauty." I think about my mother's descriptions of strolling in city parks with her cousins and girlfriends on languorous weekend afternoons as they graciously receive with covert glances and nodded heads the artfully spoken appreciation from men, still boyish, young like them, both sexes at the peak of their beauty.

O ne evening, approaching dusk, I sit with my family in the backseat of a chauffeured car driving to a restaurant. Suddenly, from the many minarets standing guard over the city, comes the call to prayer.

I learned to love this sound, this music, when on a visit to Damascus in my twenties. To me it is exotic, yes, but also soothing, powerful, sacred. I see out of the window a group of men who have answered the call and gathered to pray. These men take up the whole sidewalk and part of the street, ignoring, as if they didn't exist, the cars and pedestrians around them. I fumble with my camera, trying to position it to capture this sight. It is awesome, inspirational. En masse, twenty, maybe thirty men kneel and genuflect, lower their heads and offer their hands, palms up, in submission and gratitude. They are one before their god; they are as a single being, brought together and bonded in faith.

*A*nother day, on one of our mini-tours of the sights and sounds of Alexandria, we visited a mosque, white and carved and molded, fronting the corniche on the edge of the sea. At the main entrance, after taking picture after picture of ourselves arranged in various configurations in front of this beautiful building, I separated from my husband to enter from a different side. As we'd prepared to step inside the main door, a man had stopped me in my tracks, palm extended. This entrance, at the top of an impressive flight of stairs, was not for me. I was to enter through a different door at the side of the mosque, the one reserved for women, girls, and young children. I obliged, and found myself taking off my shoes to enter a narrow, empty space sectioned away from the main room by a latticed screen. As my bare feet sunk into the plush softness of the carpet, I noticed that I could see over this screen. It was on the other side that I saw the grandeur of the mosque's interior: the lofty ceiling, the stained glass, the intricately worked brass chandeliers casting their mosaiced light on the men praying below them.

*A*nother evening, I'm looking out the car window once again. There's a young woman leaving the university, heavy book bag on her slim shoulder. Like the girl in the palace gardens, she wears one of the uniforms common in this city: the jeans that set off the shape of her legs, the shirt that enhances a narrow waist, the long sleeves that cover the flesh of her arms, the hijab that hides her hair.

I watch as she enters a dark tunnel I imagine is also damp and isolated. Who else can be there? I see no one. She enters nonetheless in this, the twilight hour, which makes the mouth of the passageway look almost black.

Later our guide tells us that Alexandria, day and night, is safe for women and girls. They walk with the confidence that they will not be harassed or assaulted; there will be no leering, no commentary, no groping. He speaks with authority and I want to believe him, although I know he's a guide who may be performing, as guides all over the world do, the best of his culture for the foreign tourists.

*T*he year before I had my first child, I lived with my husband in Boston. There I tried to get used to the train system that was so efficient in taking people here and there from the suburbs to the city and back, from shopping centers to museums to the streets full of restaurants and cafés. On a certain afternoon, the train was crowded, so much so that I was forced to stand among other passengers squeezed in around me, one hand holding a pole for balance. As the door opened at my stop, I felt something hard press against my thigh. I noticed it almost subconsciously, intent as I was on preparing to disembark. It was only later, when walking on the platform, that I recalled the insistent hardness on my leg and finally associated it with the young man's face so close to mine before it turned away, but only after he'd made sure to catch my attention and look intently into my eyes, insisting on a further connection, on the confirmation of his act.

*O*ur guide, the one who tells us that it is safe for women and girls in Alexandria, seems to imply a blanket safety, a general physical safety. But I, with my cynical feminist mind, can't help but question. He must mean in public spaces only. He must mean women in hijab only. For otherwise, I think, how can any modern city be such a gendered utopia? Even so, what a gift, what a wonder, to move about in public, among men, without fear of the unwanted look, the unwelcome touch.

All over the streets of Alexandria, from early morning and late into the night, I saw vans driving busily back and forth, up and down. They were often full of people, commuting, erranding, moving from place to place. And I mean full. Men and women squashed together, side by side. The women, when I could see their faces through the windows as the van either flashed or crawled by, looked at ease, calm, invested in thinking or reading or being bored. Isn't this something? The freedom to be bored in a commuter van full to the brim with men?

*D*uring the hour we have to change planes at JFK on our return journey, I readjust my attitude as if pulling up a bra-strap or straightening my belt. In Egypt I worried about being judged as foreign and Western and Other, as immodest and self-sexualizing; in the United States I can be judged as not sexy enough or, at the same time, as always sexually available. It feels as if I wear a kind of hijab, a veil that can never be fully removed. I must switch from one version to the other as I switch from the first plane to the next. Yet neither of my hijabs—both of them metaphorical, ideological, and political, both imposed then learned — can protect me. Either way, I will be found lacking, far from fulfilling an impossible and shifting ideal.

Small Freedom

(*California, 2020*)

I'm shopping at the grocery store in the time of fear and contagion, in the time of masks. Habit has me checking my reflection in the narrow mirror located over the makeup section.

As I smooth down my hair, a young woman working there smiles at me and says, "You got it! You look good."

I laugh. "Why do I even bother," I say, "when I'm wearing this?" and gesture to the mask covering half my face. As I walk away, pushing my cart in front of me, I ponder my own question. Masks—like my Catholic school uniform, which blurred class lines by preventing popularity from being based on Laura Ashley dresses or Jordache jeans—can be democratizing. My mask is black, matching my daily exercise outfit (a kind of uniform itself), and it covers my main worry about my looks these post-menopausal days: wrinkles and jowls, the pull of gravity that is changing an image I've cultivated and nurtured with makeup and hairstyles and sunglasses and outfits. What do you do when your identity, the one that you've had, more or less, for the last three decades, begins to disintegrate? The mask democratizes because it hides. It hides more than half a face, it hides an image. It denigrates or enhances, according to one's perspective, nudging people closer to a common denominator. I can hide behind my mask. Not completely, but enough, enough to change the way I move about, the way I see others, the way they see me.

I think of the burqa, a type of uniform odious to me most of the time, and how it too can serve as a mask—it is the ultimate mask, hiding the whole face, the whole body. Even wrists and hands are hidden from view with long sleeves and gloves. Some burqas have black mesh to conceal the eyes, and I have also seen masks made of metal—iron or bronze—that have been molded to cover the upper face, allowing only two small openings to see through.

The burqa, I've heard argued, can be liberating. Because it hides and homogenizes. Because it says, *Hands off, this is not for you to touch or look at or consume in any way.* In this regard it is similar to the hijab, which has also been used as a tool to fashion different types of freedoms. Years ago, when my family and I were visiting Alexandria, our host told us how so many more women, young and old, had recently taken to wearing hijab. By 2006, it was seen as a symbol of resistance to the West's colonization of Egypt and the Middle East. Wearing hijab had become a political as well as a religious act, a staking with pride the claim to a non-Western culture and identity. "But," our host concluded in a confiding tone, "I think many women wear the scarf to cover their frizzy hair!" I laughed when he said this, surprised and delighted, because I'd been fantasizing since we landed in Cairo about the freedom from my unmanageable curls that the scarf could give me.

One evening on that same trip, my husband and I took our small sons to a restaurant early, at around seven o'clock. Because this was well before the usual crowds descended, the restaurant was almost empty. A young man sat at one of the two other occupied tables with a woman in full burqa beside him. They both faced away from the center of the room and so, as it happened, toward me. I watched them, fascinated as always with the handling and protocol of wearing the burqa. How would she eat? Many years earlier, at a fancy Arabic restaurant in London, I'd seen men in silk Versace shirts sitting at a table with their black-shrouded wives or sisters or mothers (I couldn't tell which), and watched how one woman took a bit of food in her gloved hand and slipped it under the front panel of her burqa to put it in her mouth. I never saw an inch, a millimeter, of flesh.

The covered woman in Alexandria proved different. Seemingly with the young man's encouragement, she lowered the front of her burqa, exposing her face in its entirety. She was young too, and so intensely pretty that I still remember her doll-like beauty—big black eyes, long lashes, full lips, a heart-shaped face. She had outlined her eyes in dark pencil and glossed her lips in pink. She giggled in her exposed state, and continued to hold with one hand the side of the face panel at the ready, as if for security. She wasn't comfortable. I got the sense that it was the young man, probably her new husband, who wanted her to take it off. Just the facial part, just for a few moments as they ate, and only because the restaurant was almost empty and her naked face was turned away from both the kitchen and the entrance. I also got the impression that he wanted to show her off—but to whom?

Perhaps, instead, he was progressively minded, and thought it silly to eat while forced to negotiate the constrictions of the burqa. Maybe she resisted, albeit mildly, his bid on her behalf for this small freedom because she had been taught all her life that she had to cover up in public, that she couldn't be a good woman, a good wife, if she exposed any part of her body once she crossed the threshold of her home. I'll never know, but that night she laughed as she ate, self-conscious, her face tucked down as if to avoid eye contact with anyone around her.

Rodeo Drive

(*Los Angeles, 2015*)

I twist my neck in the rental car, trying to see up to the top of the palm trees lining the street. My husband is driving while our sons sit in the back, so I'm free to twist and crane to my heart's content. These palms are so tall, so stately. I've seen them in dozens of ads, movies, and videos, but only a few times in real life, and never with both of my children. I'm twisting and craning because I want to really *see* them as we pass underneath, to feel, as viscerally as possible, that we're in Beverly Hills.

I have an active maternal radar, always working, always searching for potential threats, on the lookout for possible danger. This radar is on high alert this afternoon, worrying about my two teenagers. On other trips, to Lima for example, I'd worried about their drinking unboiled tap water or sitting, still toddlers, in the back of a taxi that didn't have seatbelts. In Cairo it was crossing the street, a dance with death at every attempt because none of the drivers ever paid the slightest attention to lights, signs, or possible pedestrians. Then there was Sicily's Mount Etna, with the mouth of the volcano right there, too easy, in my maternal opinion, to stumble into without a barrier or even any warnings. Today, in Los Angeles, I don't know if my sons might contract, like a virus, the rampant materialism on display, or if, naturally immune, they'll focus instead on the tiny burgers and overpriced fries their father and I buy for them on a break from sightseeing.

The restaurant is cool and dim with a dark décor—it's been remodeled so that everything is in shades of taupe and gray. The street outside is bright with sun, and sharp architectural lines cut across the blue sky. The buildings are all angles and geometric shapes, stark whites and slick chromes. In the dining room, I notice the window beside which, fifteen years prior, my older son sat hiding behind a curtain that today, due to the remodel, is no longer there. That morning long ago he peeked out at me from behind heavy drapes, smiling delightedly. As a young mother of a two-year-old, I concentrated mostly on him, and the materialism, the superficiality, the cold consumerism of the neighborhood didn't affect me the same way. I felt, back then, that I could protect him. I was in charge of his food, his clothes, his sleep, his toys—basically, of his happiness. But now this same son sits at the table, tall and lean and dark-haired, wearing size thirteen basketball shoes, his face serious. What is he thinking? These days, whenever I ask him, he says, "Nothing."

My type of motherhood makes me take everything about my sons personally. They are mine—I made them, nurtured them, fed them. One has my dark eyes, my big thighs, my aversion to conflict, the other my buck teeth (before orthodontics), my long arms, my emotional sensitivity. Both have my curly hair, my olive skin, my love of classical music. I want them to have inherited, too, my feminism. My feminism that is not about an automatic hatred of all men, or a blind idealization of all women—which is a form of objectification itself—but a humanizing feminism, one asserting that no one can be truly free until everyone is free. I want my sons to have inherited this kind of feminism, its surety and confidence, its pushback and resistance.

Outside on the patio, their chairs almost touching the window behind which we eat and drink, sit two men in their early thirties. One is clean-shaven and beginning to bald, while his companion has a head of brown hair and a dark, trendy beard. They both wear shorts and T-shirts, luxury reserved for their cell phones, their designer glasses, the champagne on ice they share in slim goblets. I watch them as they wave to women strolling by, but only the young women, only the attractive women who have glossy hair, manicured nails, and precise makeup. It's clear to me that these men, hunters on an expedition, have one goal.

As a mother, my irrational assumption is that my children have inherited, along with my DNA, the benefit of my experiences, of my learning. I tend to believe on some level that they understand the world similarly to how I do. I know this isn't true. But still, in a sort of desperate fashion, I fantasize. Why can't I shape their reactions? Why can't I translate cultural signs and signifiers to control—mother as benevolent puppet master—their experience? Back when they were two and four and six and seven, I could carry them in my arms, hold tightly onto their hands, and bark orders—Come back! Don't touch! Be careful! I could still shield their eyes, literally, at a scary scene in a movie or a distressful sight on a street.

At the restaurant we've chosen for lunch, the one in the Wilshire Hotel where pretty woman Julia Roberts stays with her prince, Richard Gere, I've brought to the attention of my family the small drama I've been following. I can see from our table inside that the men sitting on the patio right next to the window separating us have finally lured two women, young and pretty and polished, to join them for drinks and flirtation. A few minutes later one of my sons, the quieter, more serious of the two, speaks up. "Mama," he says, "the guy with the beard . . . his screensaver is a photo of a lady with two girls." He's noticed, through the window, a screensaver that looks like two daughters and their mother. I can tell from his tone of voice, cautious yet revelatory, that he knows there's something wrong with this, and the fact that my son has observed this potential sordidness pains me. I pause. Can this be true? Is this man prepared to cheat on his wife, on his daughters, on his family, with any attractive and available woman who walks by?

Most of my life I've sided with women. Automatically, no questions asked. They—we—are, ultimately, the hunted and chased and stalked, the judged and objectified, the used and abused. There are so many examples. But one memory that comes to mind because it was so random yet so normal: A man pushes a crying woman out of his car in the middle of a San Francisco street near where I walk. Bitch! He calls her. Fucking bitch! I was young then myself, the same age as my older son is today. I could only walk on, horrified, feeling powerless to intervene even if intervention was possible at that point, or to help the woman, still weeping, on the street. In this flash of history, mundane in our culture but forever reverberating in me, no one stopped to help her—no solicitous adult, no kindly older mother or grandmother, no chivalrous man.

Now I have two sons, and none of the daughters I once was so sure I would. Has this changed my feminism? No, not at its core. But yet, in some ways, yes. I now see more clearly how our culture of object versus subject, of power over rather than power to, of winner or loser damages women and men, daughters and sons, mothers and fathers.

While we finish our food and drinks we debate the meaning of the screensaver. What *can* it mean when coupled with the image of its owner (so suave and dapper) smiling and flirting with the women (both of them pretty and single) he and his companion have invited to sit with them? Worst-case scenario: wife and daughters. Best-case scenario: sister and nieces. Most improbable scenario: ex-wife and children. I, based on the evidence, believe in the cheating explanation. The four of us watch the action outside for a while longer. The boys lose interest quickly, but I can't stop brooding.

As a daughter of two beloved parents, I've felt about their future deaths anticipatory guilt, anticipatory grief. As a mother, I'm always feeling anticipatory trauma. I want to locate the danger, not only in the present, but also in the future, and steer my children clear of it. When my sons were first born, especially the older one, my husband called me maladaptive. As in not able to adapt calmly, steadily, to the worries—psychological and emotional—of motherhood. He hasn't called me that since they were toddlers, but I've recently resurrected the term in my head. Perhaps I *am* maladaptive. I can't reconcile the world around me with my relentless urge to protect my children. There's an umbilical cord, invisible, yes, but strong and robust; I feel this anticipatory trauma, this borrowed-from-an-imagined-future pain, for my sons—no matter what their age.

After some time, I leave the table in search of a restroom. While washing my hands with perfumed soap, I see reflected in the gilt-framed mirror the two young women who've joined the men from outside the restaurant and watch them, unnoticed, as they talk in a language foreign to me. They speak quickly and intensely, back and forth, standing close together. I assume they're discussing the men waiting for them. They may be debating the pros and cons of extending their time with these new acquaintances, these men who are so obviously looking for seduction and sex if not affection and friendship. At this point, are they predator or prey? Perhaps both.

I never thought, when I was young myself, that I would care, that I should care, about the boys and the men. About sons or brothers or fathers. Yet now, a shifting kaleidoscope, my perspective changes. I now see male as well as female vulnerability in this masculinist ecosystem where the fittest thrive with money, with sex and sports cars and designer sunglasses, with the predator's lens. Where does that leave the earnest and straightforward? The innocent and gullible? Where does that leave the children, all the children, *my* children?

On our way back to our car, walking on the other side of Rodeo Drive, I see old men in Bentleys and Lamborghinis with young shiny-haired wives. I see women fraxeled and fillered and botoxed. I see girls with the latest trendy handbags, phone cases, manicures, highlights. Both men and women, the models in giant airbrushed photographs displayed by skin care emporiums, hair salons, or even jewelry stores: beautiful, youthful, enviable.

I've heard that today's teenagers talk about "body counts" in tallying the number of sexual partners they've had. I've also heard the story my friend tells me: her son's first girlfriend, after talking with another girl in their high school group, accuses him of rape. Because, looking back, she didn't really want to have sex. This retrospective reluctance must mean coercion. The boy survives, although ostracized by his group, and weeks pass before the former girlfriend retracts her accusation, blaming her friend's undue influence. It's all a mess of misunderstandings and drama. But the boy is scarred. His mother laments her son's first experience with love and sex and attraction. This story happened to a real boy in real life. He will carry its weight with him forever, however heavy or light, in some way. Patriarchy with its tenets, its mythologies and its practices, is all-encompassing in its reach, limitless in its damage.

And then, there they are again. The palms. I see them from afar as we approach the street they help define as iconic. But I don't bother to crane my neck as we pass underneath them for the second time that day. I'm in a bad mood. A pall has descended on me that's about my children and this world I've brought them into, a world—I've just been reminded—saturated with vulnerability. Everything is perspective. And mine has shifted with this most recent twist of the kaleidoscope from curious and only vaguely apprehensive at the beginning of our Rodeo Drive adventure to fearfully cynical at the end. The palms look skinny and frail to me now, subject to threatening forces, easy to overpower. They lack the stateliness, the majesty they seemed to embody just three short hours ago. My mood colors my vision and they remind me not only of all the sons and daughters wanting to fit in and be loved, but also of all the mothers who want to protect them.

Kept Woman

(California, 1988–Present)

My Peruvian grandmother had a favorite and it wasn't me. Her favorite grandchild was Talia, one of my seven cousins. Talia was part of the "second batch" of children my aunt and uncle had after they learned from doctors that an older son's headaches were caused by an inoperable brain tumor, a tumor that would kill him. I've often wondered if they deliberately had three more children after hearing that news, in an attempt to compensate for the coming loss of one of their sons.

The first of this second batch, a child born to fill an unfillable void, Talia was nonetheless neglected by her parents. My aunt and uncle were too focused on the beautiful boy, the surfing teenager, the one with his mother's black eyes and easy smile, the one with his father's brown hair and broad forehead, the one who would soon die. Enter our grandmother. A longtime widow, she lived between the home shared by her three spinster sisters, where she had a room of her own, and my aunt's house, which was built with a wing especially for her. When she stayed with her daughter, in her own suite, my grandmother invariably shared her bed with Talia. She doted on this granddaughter. She cared for her and spoiled her. She put up with her restless thrashing at night; she took her to the dentist when her teeth showed signs of too much Coca-Cola and too little brushing; she gave her spoonfuls of fragrant *agua de naranja* before bed to calm her hyperactivity. She was a mother to her when Talia's own was obsessed with the health of her son.

Because of this dotage and this bond, I know my grandmother imparted the same words of wisdom to Talia as she was growing up that she gave me whenever she visited my family. I know with a confidence born of watching my grandmother raise this favorite grandchild that she told Talia at least once, but probably many times, that *una mujer no es completa sin esposo y hijos*. A woman could never be truly fulfilled without a husband and children. Born in 1906, my grandmother grew up with a South American brand of Catholicism that idealized the Virgin Mary as passive receptacle and pious intermediary. It's no wonder she believed a woman's primary purpose in life was to become a mother.

As I grew into a teenager in the United States, I started to protest this blanket definition of ideal womanhood I saw as quashing my ambitions. I knew of no one, for example, who felt that true fulfillment for boys depended on marriage and fatherhood. My long-widowed grandmother, always faithful to her doctrine of womanly happiness, dismissed my protestations with a wave of her hand, a hand increasingly wrinkled but adorned, always, with her wedding ring. She believed a woman without a husband, without children, *sin una familia*, was lacking, wanting, a puzzle with a piece missing, forever incomplete.

When Talia was sixteen, she and my grandmother visited my family in California. One spring evening, my cousin and I sat in the back of the car while my mother drove with my grandmother seated beside her. We were going to the city, to San Francisco, to have a drink at the top of the Fairmont, an iconic hotel with a glamorous history that matches its elegant décor and breathtaking views of the City and the Bay. On display, as if for our sole benefit, would be the blunt beauty of Coit Tower and the pagoda roofs of Chinatown, with the shimmer of Berkeley and Oakland in the distance.

Talia and I chatted in the dim warmth of the backseat, and somehow our conversation turned toward ambition. What did we want for ourselves? For our futures? Perhaps this conversation was triggered by the problems, related to me by my mother, that my cousin was having with her boyfriend. I was a college student then; I spoke of higher education, university degrees, and fulfilling work that would grant me independence. Talia spoke of getting married to someone rich, someone who could "take care of her" so that she wouldn't have to work and would be able, instead, to stay at home in her large house with her many handsome sons and pretty daughters. "*¡Ay, yo no!*" she said in response to my talk of having a career. "*Yo quiero casarme y quedarme en la casa con mis hijos.*" Her dream in life was to raise a family at home—with, of course, cooks, chauffeurs, and maids.

At first I was astonished by her commitment to a fate I then believed should be avoided or escaped. Only later did I realize she was speaking as a younger version of our grandmother, who believed that the pinnacle of success for a woman was an idealized maternity, a pampered domesticity. At that point, Talia had never lived outside the Peru that shaped my grandmother; she had grown up among the elite of Lima, people who felt happiness lay in frequenting hair salons and golf clubs, owning expensive high-rise apartments in the city and large estates on its periphery, and wearing Gucci, Valentino, and Cartier. Men made the money, mostly in family businesses that offered plentiful leisure time in between going to the office and making deals, while women hosted dinners and parties, attended charity luncheons and museum fundraisers, planned their children's extravagant christenings and graduations and weddings.

My surprise that night at my cousin's aspirations did not, however, prevent me from observing with envy her outfit—fitted jacket with gold buttons over a sleek matching mini skirt, sheer black hose, stiletto pumps. The frizzy-hair gene I inherited from our grandmother had somehow bypassed Talia, and her long, thick hair hung glossily over a shoulder. Although younger than me, she looked sophisticated, poised, chic.

A year later Talia was still with her boyfriend—the problematic one, the one with whom there were difficulties. I heard a disturbing story from my mother, who spoke regularly on the phone with her sister in Lima. Talia and her boyfriend were sitting in his sports car, parked somewhere outside of the gated community, among the rocky hills and sand dunes surrounding the lushly irrigated oasis that was their neighborhood. In my imagination, irrationally, Talia wore the very same outfit she did the night at the Fairmont. It was evening. It was dark. They argued. He, in a fit of pique, ordered her out of his car. She did get out, that much we knew, but after what? Disbelief? Anger? Pleading? I imagined her, my cousin, the young woman who, despite her sophisticated look, was strangely naïve, abandoned in a dark and dangerous landscape that must have felt like a desolate wasteland.

"*¿Te puedes imaginar?*" my mother tsk-tsked as she shook her head, frowning. "*¡La dejó plantada!* He left her stranded!"

My aunt was also outraged, but not enough to stop her daughter from seeing this rich young man, an eligible bachelor and a "catch." I don't know how Talia got home that night—did her boyfriend repent and return for her? Did she manage to navigate, in the high heels my imagination placed on her feet, the rocky ground to the road where she found an open restaurant or a helpful person driving by?

hen Talia was eighteen, she visited California once again, this time with her mother. She was pregnant and the problematic boyfriend refused to marry her. The extended family was keeping Talia's pregnancy from my grandmother in order to shelter her from the painful news about her favorite grandchild, which would come as a blow. We worried about *her*, about the connection in the elderly between stress and heart attacks or strokes. When they did tell her about the pregnancy, they lied and implied a wedding, a small, civil ceremony, that had already happened. My grandmother, living in Lima, increasingly confused by time and age, by rapidly growing grandchildren and great-grandchildren, by change in general and the partial diaspora of her family in particular, accepted this version of events, content to believe her beloved happy.

On that visit, again Talia and I, the first cousins, sat in the backseat as my mother drove us to lunch at a waterfront restaurant by the Bay, this time with her sister, my aunt, beside her in the passenger seat.

Our conversation in the back turned to my cousin's future, to her baby. If it was a boy, Talia told me, she would name him Julio Agusto Reyes—the same exact name as his father. Again, I was astonished; but this time I was also dismayed, outraged even. Why would she name her child after the man who'd rejected her? The man who'd mistreated her during their three years together? The entitled, spoiled, rich boy? There was no mention of independence, of ultimatums, of taking control over the situation, of disowning an uncommitted father-to-be and turning to her own family—mother, father, siblings, grandmother, aunt, cousins—who would support her and love her child. I realized she was still in the same frame of mind as before. She wanted marriage to a rich man; she expected motherhood within an expensive home, surrounded by luxury.

I quickly gathered together my imperfect knowledge of child support and child custody, of legal rights and legal obligations for a single mother of a baby. I knew she was planning to give birth in Miami, away from the prying eyes and gossiping tongues of Lima's high society. What were her rights?

"What if," I asked her, "Julio never marries you? What if you put his name on the birth certificate and christen your baby Julio Jr., and then the father comes after the child and tries to take him from you? You have to protect yourself!"

Talia dismissed my concerns. I sensed that she, sitting beside me in her maternity leggings and tunic, belly big over her thighs, considered me extreme—too serious, overly political.

Four years after giving birth, Talia was still single. Her ex-boyfriend, the father of her little boy, Julio Agusto Reyes Jr., had a new wife. This couple lived in a large house in the same gated community outside Lima where Talia grew up. Because he was rich, Julio Sr. had men who guarded him, his house, his wife, and, later, his legitimate children.

During this time, the Peruvian magazine *¡Hola!* published a dramatic spread. There were photos of my cousin clutching her little boy close to her, his skinny arms around her neck, his bare legs around her torso. There were police cars in the background, with flashes of red and blue lights caught by the camera's lens, frozen forever in time. There were people everywhere on this beachfront property up the coast from the city.

I remember poring over the article that titillatingly described the events leading to these photographs: The kidnapping of the child from the home of his mother and grandparents. The use of armed bodyguards. The sequestering of the child at the father's beach house. The rescue of the child by police and the reunion with his mother. It was all pandemonium, all drama; it looked like anarchy. Talia got her son back, but at what price?

Fast-forward fifteen years. My grandmother is dead. She has gone, yes, but not before meeting my husband and approving of my choice, not before seeing my firstborn and approving of his birth. She became acquainted with my husband before she died, and she delighted in his confidence, his rudimentary but careful Spanish, his family's affluence. I have a photograph of her with my infant son. Taken when we traveled to Peru to visit family, in this picture my baby is five months old. He reclines on a sofa next to his great-grandmother. She—in a gesture that reminds me irresistibly of Michelangelo's portrayal of God reaching out to Adam—delicately, almost warily, extends a finger toward him, smiling. Delicately, because she is, as always, dressed in silk and alpaca, her long strand of pearls hanging heavily from her neck, the familiar diamonds on her hands, her silver hair up in its signature bun. Her movements seem to have a certain precision in my memory, her manicured fingers are careful, economical. Warily, because she, I realize only as an adult, did not like children. Although she valued the *idea* of children as "completing" a woman, as giving a woman purpose and respect, for real, live children who were not her favorites, she had little time and less patience.

In this photograph my small son smiles back with his eyes as well as his mouth—with eyes that are dark, like mine, like my mother's, like my grandmother's—almost as if he knows her the way I do, intimately, her quirks and flaws, her strength and humor; as if—true to the fresco in the Sistine Chapel, I like to think—there's a spark between them.

Only lately, in my forties and early fifties, am I becoming aware of how I too have internalized my grandmother's precepts, her teachings, her example, her doctrine. Even though I educated myself, earning my final degree at the age of thirty-two, my grandmother's ambitions (as well as those of my mother, who inherited them fully and unproblematically) were always present, an inescapable pressure that hovered around me, coloring my thoughts, influencing my decisions. The things they wanted and expected for me—to marry and marry well, to become a wife, cared for and secure, and then a mother, needed and fulfilled—were in some shape or form, I understand now, always my own aspirations, merely buried under the surface. More recently, as I follow in many of both my grandmother's and mother's footsteps, it has been my children who have filled my thoughts, defined my goals, and held my heart.

Today, eleven years after my grandmother's death, Talia's son is an adult who was brought up solely, in the end, by his mother and her parents. Talia, meanwhile, lives in Miami, a continent away from Lima and the father of her only child, working full time. She has worked for decades because she has had to. She failed in fulfilling her dreams and accomplishing her goals. Although she is lately married, it is a marriage that reneged on its promise of happily-ever-after and became instead a punishment, a sacrifice. She is married to a man much older than her, a man who could be her father, a man who was rich at their wedding but became impoverished after a few years by an infamous pyramid scheme. She held the fairy tale, her dream, her ambition, in her hand for a moment, like a perfect golden bowl, only to see it fissure and crack through no fault of her own.

And I? I worked in the past because I wanted to. I don't work any longer; I gave up a career in research and teaching. Marriage, domesticity, and especially motherhood became too complicated, too demanding. I chose a maternal identity over a professional one; this has been my sacrifice as a mother and a woman, as well as an academic and a feminist. The decision was painful—messy, long, and drawn out. It wasn't one that I made in a single moment, in one place, or through one epiphany, but over time, with experience, in the face of new, sometimes unexpected, realities. I've found since then that there is great truth in my grandmother's words: motherhood has been fulfilling. But also . . . consuming. Consuming in the powerful, overwhelming, *enthralling* sense of the word. In my experience it left little space for other concerns, for projects or work, for any substantial time away from my children.

Thus if my cousin's story is a failed fairy tale, a warped telenovela, then mine is a tale of concession and compromise. Although I consider myself educated and intellectual, there has been, undoubtedly, a trade-off. These days I think to myself, *Who is the kept woman now?*

Part Four

❧

HARVESTING

Wrinkles

(Peru and California, 2020)

I'm looking at a photograph taken by an iPhone in Lima and sent to me in California. It shows my aunt and uncle sitting in their living room on their low cream couch, a leopard print cushion in the corner and an antique oil painting of the Archangel Rafael in rusts and reds and golds hanging behind them. I wouldn't have thought that the animal print would go with the Catholic imagery, but it does; the luxury of the colors and the historical undertones—gilt frame, papal riches, safari hunting—brings it all together in an edgy way that seems right to me, having grown up surrounded by the aesthetics of Spanish colonialism.

This one I save to my phone album because I know I will want to return to it time and again, especially when my aunt and uncle are gone. They are, as of the taking of this picture, eighty-seven and ninety-two years old, respectively. They sit close to each other, as is their wont, embodying what I consider to be one of the great love stories in my family, if not the only one. They lean into one another, and her hand presses his as it rests on his leg.

I grew up watching my aunt touch my uncle constantly, sitting next to him at the dining table for instance, rubbing his arm and plucking his skin gently with her thumb and forefinger as she talked to my mother—pluck, smooth, pluck, smooth, pluck, smooth. Once when we were teens my sister entered their room without knocking to ask a question after everyone had retired for the night; she found them in bed gazing into one another's eyes and caressing each other's faces. Who does that at sixty-plus years old? After forty-plus years of marriage and seven children?

But what strikes me about this particular photo is my aunt. Of course I notice that she's elegantly dressed, her hair styled, a dramatic silver necklace around her throat. That is normal. What is also normal, but what I end up still mulling over later, is her face. It is wrinkled. She has the kind of skin that shows its age in webs of fine lines, especially around her eyes and mouth. She is an animated talker, charismatic and exuberant, and when she laughs or smiles her mouth moves and her eyes crease. A lot. My mother, her younger sister, is less dramatic. She is quieter, shyer, more self-conscious. Her face has moved less, let's put it that way. And her skin is different, thicker, less fragile. My mother has hardly any fine lines.

Growing up, I spent weeks and sometimes months of my school vacations in Lima, visiting my Peruvian family. Like my mother, I am more quiet and shy than my aunt, and was especially so as a child. Often, instead of playing or even reading, I watched my aunt and observed her style, noting how she talked and moved, what she wore, how she decorated her house and instructed servants. One of her favorite hobbies around that time was gardening. She loved her garden—creating it, tending to it. She loved ordering the gardeners around, telling them where to dig ditches and holes, how to plant the palms and ferns and acacias. She also loved watering the trees and flowers. This love she shares with my mother and me. As an adult I've realized how we three share the satisfaction of wielding a hose, adjusting its nozzle, giving water to thirsty plants and grass that will take that water and thrive, populating our surroundings with texture and color and scent.

I can see my aunt in my mind now—much younger, maybe forty-five years old. She rolls up her slacks and steps out onto her lawn with a long hose that unfurls as she walks. She waters as she goes, paying special attention to the ferns and orchids that fill the shadier corners. If a gardener crosses her path, she gesticulates toward the jobs she wants done. Her feet are bare but her hands stay adorned with diamond rings and gold bracelets. Although her hair is done and her face made up, she is not fastidious like her oldest daughter or even her mother; she keeps her nails short, and her hands are strong and broad— the better to play the piano, comfort a child, or repot a flower. I once watched her jump into a pool, clothes and jewelry and all, to rescue a flailing toddler; I can still see her tanned hand clasping his arm as she lifted him to safety.

All this is to say that my aunt has spent much of her time outdoors. Not just in the garden, watering and supervising and repotting, but also at the beach or the pool. She has much lighter skin than my mother, which was part of the familial narrative of her superior beauty when she and my mother were growing up. When she was young, my aunt was fair-skinned and dark-haired like a South American Vivien Leigh. Maybe she took this beauty for granted, having been assigned it since infancy, but in any case she never cared about the sun, about getting brown or freckled. Most of the summers in the period of time I'm recalling, in her middle age when she lived in a gated community with a large, lush garden and plenty of irrigation, she got darker, lightening again during the mild winters, marking the seasons with her skin tone. In the warm months she often wore bright *pareos* from morning to night, tied around the top of her chest and over her bathing suit. My mother, on the other hand, never liked to tan, always conscious of the stigma of being too brown to begin with. And now, looking at the photograph, I can see the consequences of my aunt's blithe attitude toward the sun. Although the bones of her particular beauty are still evident—her nose delicate, her cheekbones sharp—her thin skin is spotted and lined.

*M*y aunt lives in an epicenter of plastic surgery. Many cities in South America—Bogotá, Caracas, Rio— promote, through a combination of pressure and propaganda, the relentless beautification of women. In Lima my aunt is surrounded by women who get fillers and Botox, lasers and peels, facelifts. Yet she has done nothing. She remains a cosmetic procedure virgin. It seems odd in someone who appears so superficial, who values designer handbags and perfumes, Italian shoes, and penthouse apartments. She constantly comments on other people's wealth, the companies and property they own, their houses and cars, as well as their looks. About a friend's daughter, for example, who is particularly pretty, she'll make sure to report several times, *"Está linda—¡preciosa!"* Is she indifferent to cosmetic work because she was considered beautiful her whole life? Because she found her husband and had her children young, at the peak of her beauty? Or perhaps this indifference stems from her distrust of doctors in general. She once told a daughter who was six months pregnant not to worry about giving birth—*"no tengas miedo."* Prenatal care wasn't necessary because having a baby was like having a tooth pulled—*"como sacarse una muela."*

Her mother, my grandmother, was not a beauty, but she was attractive enough to catch the eye of the Italian gentleman who had emigrated from Genoa, and all her life she looked elegant in silk, heels, and her signature pearls. My grandmother escaped the era of plastic surgery, of chemical and surgical alteration of the body and the face. She never dyed her hair, but instead wore it swept up in a large bun that over the years turned from black to gray to white. Growing up, I never noticed her aging face; it was just a normal part of her, an essential aspect of her character. I never thought to criticize it, or to imagine how she could fix it to look better. What I noticed instead was the way her black eyes crinkled when she laughed, how her silver hair framed her wide cheekbones, how her broad smile exposed slightly protruding teeth.

My mother, though, gave in to the siren call of cosmetic surgery, with its promises of prolonged youth, a thinner body, a firmer face. Why did she and not my aunt? Why did she, when she was used to decades of being in the shadow of a brilliant sister? Used to being the darker, plainer one? Maybe it was because of this. Maybe she saw surgery as her opportunity to shine, to transform from an ugly duckling into a shimmering swan.

To be clear, my mother, my beautiful aunt's little sister, is not ugly, or even plain. She is also beautiful, but in a quiet, unassuming way. And everything is relative. Raised in Peru with a sister whose beauty was striking, whose looks called out and demanded attention, taught my mother that she was wanting, that she lacked charm and attraction, that she was the drab, homely side of the coin.

She likes to tell a story about her First Communion: My grandmother dressed both her daughters in the requisite white—veil, dress, gloves, even rosary—and, as if they were twins, had them take their first communion together. At the party afterward, none of the guests remembered my mother, instead passing her over to congratulate her older sister and give her the gifts they had brought. My mother remembers, much more clearly than the actual ceremony at the church, feeling invisible, ignored, excluded. Her sister, once again, shone with the light of the sun, leaving my mother in the shadows. After all, it was just my mother and my aunt: two sisters, born close enough in time so that they were constantly compared — not quite twins, but almost.

In the ten years leading to her facelift, my mother had become dumpier; she had gained weight around her middle, and her clothes had begun to reflect her insecurities about aging. Because she was conveniently in Lima visiting her sister, because her children were grown and no longer her daily responsibility, and because the cost of the surgery was a bargain, the siren call proved too seductive. She decided to go for it, paying for the procedure out of her own pocket money, and the accommodating surgeon threw in liposuction and a tummy tuck.

On the phone the morning after, when she was recovering at my aunt's house, she sounded weak and miserable. She told me, in a slow, slurring whisper, that she had never endured such pain in her entire life. That she hurt all over, but especially around her stomach. As if rebelling against its cute name, the tummy tuck had turned vicious.

My sister and I were worried about the whole situation. About our mother in Peru, so far away from us in California, undergoing a serious operation under anesthesia. And one so unnecessary. What if something went wrong? We knew what had happened to the founder of the original "First Wives Club" — who, after writing about being cast aside by her husband for a younger, prettier woman, died on the operating table during a facelift. Plus, for a fraction of the price in the United States, could the surgeon possibly be a good one? What if he was a hack?

But my mother, after two weeks of pain and healing in Lima, recovered.

I remember driving with my sister to the airport in San

Francisco to pick our mother up. It was during the days when you could walk straight to the gate. When she emerged from the jet bridge we almost didn't recognize her. We were met with a marvel, a vision. We had dropped off a mother with a thickening waist and a softening face, wearing a chunky, hand-knit sweater. We picked up a sophisticated woman, outfitted in camel-colored slacks and a silk top with matching heels. Her waist was narrow, her figure svelte. She'd had her hair done so that highlights shone in the same sexy cut she'd sported when young and single. And her face! She easily looked forty, a good twenty years younger than her actual age.

I was so happy for her. I loved her new look. My sister, however, confessed to me later that she missed her "old mom"— the comfortable one, the more obviously maternal one. Our mother as a gorgeous, glamorous woman felt alien to her.

I n California the pressure on women to look good is also palpable: we should present a certain ideal, a femininity that is thin and toned, as well as perky-breasted, smooth-skinned, and full-lipped. In certain circles, the cosmetically altered look, with fillers and lifts and lasers, feels more normal. Bleached teeth, Fraxeled skin, and Botoxed foreheads are common. When I go from a morning walk with my friend who eschews most cosmetic indulgence beyond sunscreen and eyeliner to afternoon coffee with friends who are more looks-conscious, I feel like an old hag in comparison with their smooth, artificially maintained faces. That very word—*hag*—comes too easily to mind, showing the degree to which I have internalized a loathing of the feminine when it's not up to the patriarchal standards (young and taut) of the male gaze.

What does it mean for my aunt to be able to leave all that to the side?

About ten years ago, she came out to California to help tend to my mother after she had a car accident. At the hospital, wrongfully assuming the relationship between them, a nurse referred to my mother as my aunt's daughter. Reminders of her diminishing looks and increasing age must have been common these past few decades. Yet my aunt feels she is enough, more than enough, in her own eyes and in the eyes of her husband, her children, her family. She rejects the conflation of *looking* younger with *being* better.

Thus even after she witnessed her little sister's dramatic transformation, my aunt did not get a facelift. She seemed Odysseus who could see the sirens on the shore, who could hear their irresistible song from the ship on the undulating ocean, yet, tied to a mast, did indeed resist the temptation to look younger and thinner, to smooth out skin and erase lines, to lighten spots and suction away fat. How was it that she seemed to wear this invisible armor without a chink, this chain mail that protected her from the dermatologist's laser and the surgeon's knife? I think it might have something to do with the great love, *el gran amor*, she shared with her husband. He refused surgery for his beloved wife and life companion, even as her beauty began to be compromised by time and gravity and sun. He was scared for her. Why should she take such a risk for something so trivial? It seems that deep down he loved *her*—her essence and her core—not just her beauty.

My aunt and uncle married when she was but seventeen and he twenty-three. She never finished high school. Instead, the young couple relocated to an *hacienda* his family owned a day's drive from the city. Since then, they have always been together, seeking each other like homing pigeons; to this day, like magnets, they become uncomfortable when pulled apart too long.

Early in their marriage, my uncle went to North Carolina

for a year to complete a degree in agriculture. Before a month passed he called for his wife to come to him. Without her, he couldn't sleep and broke out in hives. In less than a week she arranged for her two young children to stay in Lima with her mother and sister and flew to the States to be with her husband.

Much later, on our yearly visits, my uncle often acted as our chauffeur, driving us here and there and waiting patiently for us in the car, dropping us off at a ladies' lunch or picking us up from the *peluquería* where we got our hair and nails done. Even last year, too old for chauffeuring, if my aunt took my mother and me shopping at Lana, the alpaca store, or at Ilaria for silver jewelry, my uncle would call her cell phone wanting to know where she was and when she would return to the house: "*¿Dónde estás? ¿Cuándo regresas?*" Although she seemed to be having fun, browsing among the silken scarves or hammered urns, my aunt always hurried home to make sure my uncle had his lunch: "*Quiero darle su almuerzo a mi Josito,*" she'd insist. "*Está muy flaquito.*"

The siren song, then, has never had power over her, *could* never have power over her, although she was exposed to it, although its music has surrounded her every day as she's grown older and technology has continued to advance. For her, the song of beautification and resurrected youth falls flat—she has what she wants, what she needs, what she deserves: the unconditional love of her most beloved.

Names

(California, 2021)

ames have constantly been on my mind, even if only at the back of it, ever since my early twenties when I started seriously seeing the man who eventually became my husband. But recently, almost thirty years since our wedding, I've started again to think more consciously about names—surnames, maiden names, married names.

Two weeks ago, I officiated the wedding of a dear sister/niece/daughter/friend of mine. I call her this because she hadn't been related to me at all until the ceremony—when, in an intricate chain involving sisters- and brothers-in-law, I became officially related to her by marriage. Nonetheless I feel I've had a hand in raising her; for years I was a kind of coparent with her mother and father, babysitting her from when she was just eight weeks old to when she was a young teenager. Since then my role has transitioned from physical caregiver and safekeeper to mentor/aunt, and then to what I feel I am today: sister/friend.

About a month ago, Adeline, this sister/friend, asked if I would officiate her legal wedding, if I would obtain a license online and put together a few words to say on the day we—a small group of very close friends and family—gathered at my parents' house down the road from mine and next door to her childhood home. That is one of the reasons she asked to have the ceremony at my parents' house, because she'd grown up running up and down the long driveway and through the iron gate to that house, feeling almost as much at home there as in her own. She grew up calling my mother her "fake grandma," in a half-joking attempt to name their relationship with a kind of shorthand, reluctant to go through the whole lineage of her relationship with our family when introducing any one of us to a friend or acquaintance. Nowadays my mother is still to her "my fake grandma," and I've been called by others, at different times, mother, aunt, and sister. Adeline used to correct people when they made such assumptions, but now rarely does. She feels, as I do, that each of those names applies in spirit, if not in fact.

On the afternoon of the wedding, I drove the few minutes down the hill from my house to my parents'. Next to me on the passenger seat lay the license the online ministry company had mailed me after I answered a few questions and paid a few dollars, as well as a copy of the speech I'd crafted from different templates and words of my own. I'd changed into what my sons like to call one of my "fancy" outfits: maroon skirt and top, high heels, gold cuff.

There had been vague, brief talk about names before the day of the ceremony, and I'd gotten the impression Adeline was going to keep her own last name, the one that for her entire life she'd shared with her late, beloved father. But I didn't recall specific decisions about the last names of any future children, except perhaps for the facetious suggestion of combining the couple's individual surnames into a blended one for their future family to share.

Standing before this young pair at the ceremony in my maroon outfit and high heels, I could have been more serious about their future plans regarding names. But I wasn't. I was too anxious about getting the ceremony right, about saying the words I had written beforehand correctly and with love and dignity, about not messing things up. I felt heavily the responsibility of the moment.

At one point, a few sentences in, I turned to look at the groom and saw with some surprise that tears had formed in his eyes. I reached out to him, touching his arm, feeling the wool crêpe of his navy-blue jacket beneath my hand. I wanted to comfort him, even if wordlessly, or rather to celebrate with him, to sympathize and rejoice with him, because he was marrying this woman, this sister/friend of mine, this wonderful human being. Now, just a few weeks later, I wonder if I should have been as sensitive to their name decision as I was to his spontaneous emotion.

Years ago, maybe thirty-two or thirty-three, my boyfriend and I sat at the bar of a restaurant, wrangling over future names. Mine for sure, then—for a tiny instant—his, then our hypothetical children's. Not first names, at that point in time, just last. Would I change my name, was the question at hand, when we did marry? Would I want to? Should I, regardless of personal desire, because it was my duty as a woman and a wife? This point was easily resolved, as my boyfriend was raised by a mother who was a physician, and who kept her maiden name as part of her professional persona. This, as he informed me, was common among the educated classes in the Middle East.

"But," I pointed out, aided and abetted by my feminist sense of justice, "what about the children? You have your father's and not your mother's last name." I wanted to know why should my children—the babies I would carry in my own body, whom I would create with my flesh and blood and bone —be solely his in name. I didn't see the justice, the fairness in having them forever identified through their father's familial lineage, and with my—their mother's—legacy relegated to obscurity, erased from their history by a tradition of patrilin-eality.

This turned out to be the sticking point.

My boyfriend, feeling confident in his feminism because of the implicit support he'd always given his mother in keeping her maiden name, couldn't stomach the idea of having his children bear any name other than his own. Hence the wrangling. Every alternative I suggested, my boyfriend shot down. What about a hyphenated name for the whole family? *No.* What about combining our names into a new one for all of us? *No.* What about a brand-new surname with some kind of meaning that we decide on for ourselves? *No.*

After a while, tired of these negotiations—which, at the time, were more for principle's sake than for practical purposes (this was years before we actually got married, let alone had children)—I suggested flipping a coin. To me, this was the ultimate fair solution. The name would be decided by chance, a kind of fate. If we were rejecting (as I was) the traditions of our time and culture, the ones that stand in for fate and destiny, the ones that replace a specific answer from a directly petitioned oracle, then we would have to substitute the petition to an oracle with a game of chance, with the flip of a coin and the calling-out, midair, of heads or tails. But again came his answer—*No.*

His objection, I imagine, lay in the horror of losing the coin toss, in having to keep his promise to have his children bear their mother's last name. Equally untenable to him was the idea of changing his name to mine in order to share it with those children. But, my argument went, isn't that what women do all the time? Isn't that what is expected of them? The sacrifice of an identity that has been theirs from birth until the moment they say "I do"?

We tabled the discussion that night with this question unanswered, with the name issue unresolved. We left it at the bar for the time being, among our emptied glasses of wine and water, alongside the dollar bills and unflipped coins that served as tips for the bartender, squeezed in among the peanut bowls and crumpled napkins.

$\mathcal{M}$y friend Kay kept her last name when she married. She and her husband planned to change their individual surnames to one family name once they had their first child. They solved the conundrum of choosing between her name and his, between a hyphenated name or a combination of their two last names, by deciding to call their family "Madrone," after their residential address. Their neighborhood was a fairly forested one, where redwoods dominated, and most streets were named after various kinds of native trees. Kay and her husband lived on Madrone Street and loved the sound and romance of the name. They fantasized together about adopting it as their own for their future family.

Remembering this egalitarian dream is bittersweet for me, because they divorced well before any children were conceived. In hindsight, I'm glad Kay still had her own surname, a separate identity, because by the end of the marriage her husband had become abusive. I found out when she was divorcing him that he'd tried to control and manipulate her—to possess her, body and soul. I'm gratified to know she never was completely his, if only in that her name remained her own.

Another friend did change her name when she married, and used to get defensive if I asked about it, saying she wasn't close to her father anyway, and therefore not attached to his name. But she now admits she regrets her decision. She says she was pressured not so much by her fiancé, but by a culture (patriarchal) and subculture (he was in the military) that found it odd, unloving, *unnatural* for a woman to keep her last name. But she's matured within the marriage, alongside and despite it, and now no longer views her husband as the strong, confident foil to her own, sometimes insecure, self. Any element of idol worship or starstruckness that may have been part of her ceding to the tradition of trading her name for his is gone, vanished, replaced by a much more clear-eyed practicality. She sees his faults and his flaws these days, as well as his strengths—but also, crucially, she sees her own strengths, strengths she wishes she had continued to own through the name she identified with her entire life until the moment she signed on the dotted line.

One of the friends I made in university "hated" her father— an emotion that covered, as it often does, a deep hurt. He first neglected her after his divorce from her mother, then favored a second daughter from a subsequent marriage. She once told me about feeling so proud and happy when her father came to one of her violin recitals—for he'd never done so before—only to realize months later that he came not for her, but for her teacher, a single, young, and attractive woman. This music teacher later became the mother of her half-sister, the one her father doted on like he never did my friend, taking photos of this second daughter as she grew up, attending her recitals and games, being at home for dinner, loving her mother. As a result, when my friend met her beloved boyfriend in college, she— eager to officially ally herself with the person to whom she had already dedicated her entire self, physically and emotionally— couldn't wait to marry him and change her name to his. She has not regretted it.

So what did I do regarding names and identity, name-changing and marriage? What happened to the discussion tabled years before my wedding to my boyfriend? I did keep my own name, my maiden name, the name I'd identified with all my life. There was no need for further talk, negotiation, or argument. That was settled as far back as the night we sat together negotiating at the bar.

The one mild pushback at this decision came from my father. For the first years of my marriage, which were before the easy communication of email or even the taken-for-granted access to personal computers, my father used to address his letters to me with "Mrs." followed by my husband's name, *first and last*. This was deliberate, each and every time, and I thought it mostly amusing. That label, which, to me, erased my entire identity, felt like a patriarchal tantrum, and in some ways it was—my father, the paterfamilias, the ostensible patriarch of our family, accustomed to getting his way in matters most important to him, on some fundamental level protested a change that upended his worldview: women must take on their husband's name in order to bear children who would represent their husband genetically *and* nominally. My father finally gave up this war, fought on the most miniscule of battlefields—an envelope—or maybe he never did, and the advent of email only fooled me into assuming so.

But what about the children? What name was written down, as if etched in stone, on our first son's birth certificate? Reader, it was my husband's . . . and mine.

We landed on a hyphenated name, on the linking forever of both our surnames, so that each would be equally official, equally valid and recognized. I don't remember any one conversation that decided this; there is no memory of a particular moment at a bar, on a walk, or in a car. It seems it was an evolution of influences and conversations and understandings.

When the matter had been settled between us and I was pregnant with my first child, a pronouncement of my obstetrician reinforced my personal stake in my children's surname as their first home, as incubator and protector and nurturer. My husband, he whose sole contribution to the creation of the fetus developing in my womb was the millions of sperm donated in a single moment, laughed inordinately at the description my doctor gave of that same fetus when I insisted he call her to find out if the baby was suffering because I could eat just a few bites of a cracker and drink a few sips of 7 Up a day.

Oh no, assured the doctor, a fetus will take everything it needs from the mother's body, if necessary even calcium directly from her bones. "A fetus," she finished with a flourish, "is a *parasite*."

My husband laughed and laughed, even as he covered the mouthpiece of the phone with his hand. To this day, the thought of our son as a greedy, grasping freeloader makes him chuckle.

It turns out our fears—that my husband's parents would be outraged by the subordination of their son's patrilineal rights, that my parents would be confused by the flouting of tradition, that our children would resent the difference or the awkwardness, were unfounded, every one. I haven't regretted keeping my name even as a married woman, as a wife. I haven't regretted my husband keeping his as a married man, as my spouse. And neither have I regretted insisting that our children inherit both their parents' surnames. Instead, I celebrate. I celebrate their identification with their father *and* their mother through their one, hyphenated last name.

On the Beach

(California, 2021)

Recently I walked on the beach, alone. But I didn't *go* to the beach alone. Instead, I went with my family as part of an annual vacation to the small town on the Pacific called Carmel-by-the-Sea. I had almost all of them with me when we first parked our three cars by the roadside: my mother and father, my sister and brother with their spouses, my niece and two nephews, and one of my sons.

I never go to the beach alone. Not, in any case, to the kind of beach common in Northern California, where there may be just a handful of other people enjoying the sun, fishing, or, if dogs are allowed, watching a Labrador or terrier run on the sand. I don't have a dog, and am too scared of a random predator (human and male) to risk parking my car in an empty lot, clambering down a rocky path alone, and taking a solitary walk up and down a desolate coastline.

Once, while sitting together on a shared picnic blanket, a friend and I watched a man walking on the deserted beach. By himself he climbed a craggy mound of boulders, high up toward the sky, until he reached the top and stood silhouetted against the bright blue, looking out away from us, toward the horizon. I've only ever seen a single woman walking on that kind of beach completely alone, without at least one other person (like me with my friend), and this woman had two massive German Shepherds with her.

Some people might suggest I go alone anyway, in this way overcoming my fear and, if lucky, also attaining a sense of self-sufficiency or empowerment. Our culture speaks of women and girls who take risks like these as daring and intrepid, mavericks of some kind, but these are abstractions that gloss over the physical stakes of harassment, assault, rape, and murder. I take umbrage not with individual women who try to seize agency, to force freedom by walking or hiking or traveling alone, but with the culture that makes doing so a gamble with one's body and life, with the sanctity of self. I could choose to go alone to a crowded beach or park, but what would be the point? The moment of privacy within nature, immersed in and surrounded by sea and sky or mountains and forest, is a small miracle to me. But I can't do it alone; it's too dangerous. I have to depend, instead, on my husband, or one of my sons, or a close friend.

When we first convened in Carmel, my fifteen-year-old niece reported that she'd just participated in an anti-rape protest in Monterey. She was beaming with the high of having taken part in something greater than oneself, of having acted upon shared values with a group of like-minded people. She showed me the palms of her hands — "Look!" — where she still had paint stains from making signs and writing slogans: *My Dress Doesn't Mean Yes. NO Means NO. Punish Rapists, not Victims! Girls are Human Beings. Enough is Enough — STOP RAPE.*

I take advantage of my family being at the beach with me to leave them almost immediately. I want to walk alone. There are a few other families as well as couples on this beach; it is by no means deserted. I also feel safe because no matter where I am on this half-crescent of sand, my family can see me; even if I walk far out of their earshot, I will always be within their eyesight.

I walk down toward the Pacific, toward the white waves endlessly breaking against the shore, gaining their momentum from the dark depths beyond. I walk away from my family, who have settled themselves in their various ways by digging in the sand, passing a football, or relaxing on folding chairs. I walk all the way down from the top of the beach's incline to the spot where the sand has been tamped down by the final, thinning reach of foamy swell into a firmness that hardly gives way under me as I step heel-ball-toes, heel-ball-toes. I walk with long strides, my hands in my jacket pockets, my face angled to the right, toward the water and the seagulls and the horizon. As I walk, I appreciate what I don't often get to feel: the breeze carrying the smell of salt and seaweed, the sun soft on my face, wet grains rough on the soles of my feet.

There's a small river ahead of me running from some unseen inland source toward the sea. Two banks of sand, gritty minicliffs, flank the water as it rushes to meet the ocean. A man who's been walking ahead of me—my double, as it were, and also my complement—stops at the edge of a bank near where the rushing river is about to meet the oncoming waves and be welcomed by the mother-sea. He's yin to my yang, or vice versa, because he's been walking alone, gazing at the waves, the ocean, the horizon. His hands are in the pockets of his rolled-up khakis. But he is male and short-haired and, also unlike me (who has on leggings and a T-shirt, as well as a pullover, puffy jacket, and scarf), wearing nothing besides the rolled-up pants and a short-sleeved shirt. Before I reach him, he's walked up along the small river and is contemplating another spot where the water is less active but the space between banks is not only much wider, but also much deeper.

I stand near the waves where he stood a minute or two ago and stare down at the rushing water. I debate the danger in my head. The gorge is narrow and shallow, but the water is surging past and I'm scared of currents that can knock a person over and drag her out to the sea where riptides will take over, making it impossible to get back to firm land. Just this past winter, a fourteen-year-old boy died on this very coast, an hour north from where I stand, when a sneaker wave surprised him and carried him out past the breakers, too far from the shore for saving.

At one point, I slide down the little embankment until I can put one foot into the water. It feels too strong. I pull out and half jump, half crawl, back up to safety.

I decide to walk to the place where the lone man is still gazing at the water that has to be crossed in order to get to the other side, where there is more of the wild coastline, as well as dramatic outcroppings of large rocks with tide pools in between. I'm not afraid of him. I sense that, like me, he wants to reach the other side, to explore that greater wildness. He also seems pleasant enough, and there are people within reach were I to feel threatened. If I'd found myself truly alone and seen a male figure ahead of me, however, I would have turned around and aborted my excursion. That's the level of my caution, a caution some call paranoia, but one fed by the fear I've been taught by the countless examples—in the news and through accounts, first- and second-hand from relatives and friends—of women hurt by men.

When I reach him, he doesn't look up. "Forget about it," I say. "You'd have to *swim* to make it across!"

He turns to me, his face quizzical.

I repeat what I've just said. "To get across here you'd have to swim!"

He's still looking at me, but says, "No English. No understand."

233

I detect an accent I recognize. *"Estoy diciendo,"* I explain, this time in Spanish, *"que si quieres cruzar, vas a tener que nadar."* I smile to make sure he knows my intentions are friendly.

He smiles back, a broad smile, signaling relief and good humor. He gets my joke.

I convince him the best way to attempt the crossing is down below, closer to the coastline and nearer the breaking waves, where the waterway is narrower and shallower. Back at the original site, where he and I both stood at our different times, we look once again at the rushing water.

"Tal vez es demasiado difícil," he says. It might be too difficult.

"No quiero morir," I say—I don't want to die—again joking.

Finally he jumps down, after telling me (also joking) that if he doesn't make it, I'll know not to attempt the crossing myself. I watch him hop high and fast over the water, not resting in one place long enough for the current to take hold of a leg and drag him out. It works. His calf muscles tense and bulge. Right before he lands on the other embankment, I jump in, almost without thinking. I laugh as I stumble a little at the end, and he reaches out to grab my arm and take my waist in order to steady my landing. We laugh together then, in triumph.

I've felt a pull, an attraction. It's part of a nostalgia, a sadness for what has gone with the passage of time and disappeared with my youth. There once was another young man—more of a boy, really. This boy I met in Manta, a resort town in Ecuador also by the beach. But my memory of that place, almost forty years ago now, is not of sand, water, or sky, but of a balcony at the back of the hotel, overlooking a carpark. Even at night it was warm. My arms were bare and my feet sandaled; sconce lights attracted insects. Leaning against the thick wooden balustrade, the boy and I performed the age-old ritual of flirtation. The humid air swelled with innuendo as his broad brown hand inched closer to mine on the railing. Lips half smiling, he asked me suggestive questions. The silences were pregnant with meaning. He pushed, I deflected. He was leading, as if we were dancing a waltz, because I was new to this. The boy, who at seventeen was almost three years older than me, was the expert.

The young man at the beach in Carmel, now behind me because I've deliberately moved away from him to allow for the privacy we both sought earlier on our solitary walks, reminds me of the boy in Manta. He sounds like him, for one thing. His accent is South American. His shirt, I now know, having seen it up close, is a fútbol jersey. His skin is brown all over, and I can tell not just from the sun. His black hair is longish at the top, cut close at the nape of the neck and around small ears. His face is thin, and handsome in a quiet way. My attraction to the young man here is but a faint echo, however, of the pull I felt for the boy in Manta, and our exchange on this beach in California but the palest of shadows flitting across this latter stage of my life, of the conversations, heavy with the promise of touch and caress, I had with the teenage boy so many years ago.

Reaching a hill of boulders that from farther away looked smooth in a homogenous gray, I try to climb it in order to access a wider view but give up after a couple of hesitant steps, defeated by the sharp surface that threatens to cut my feet. Walking back, I see the young man standing below among the black rocks, staring down at the water as it floats in and out of the spaces between outcroppings with the force of the waves, pooling in rhythmic intervals around his ankles. The taupe of his still rolled-up khakis matches the color of the sand, the green of his jersey matches the tones of the emerald sea. Even his skin, a soft brown, comes close in color to the scattered patches of bronzed lichen on the stones. *He's practically camouflaged*, I think. He looks as if he belongs here, a natural part of the landscape.

I have an urge to take a photo of him, obtain his address (wherever it is—Venezuela, Colombia, Argentina?), and send him a copy. It's hours before I realize I wouldn't have had to ask for a residential address; this is, after all, 2021 and there are such things as the cell phone with which I was planning to take the picture in the first place. I just needed his number. But that might have seemed like some kind of misguided flirtation, which wasn't my intention. What I really wanted, I only understood later, was to photograph that scene—the man staring at the sea, standing among the rocks so naturally, so organically—and thus memorialize it forever as an image on a screen.

The attraction I felt to this young man, which I've since pondered thoroughly, was not romantic or sexual; it was not all maternal (my two sons are just now reaching adulthood); and it was not the passing interest of a native for a tourist. He had in him, I could sense if not see, a quality of vulnerability, and in some ways I was the stronger: resident to his foreigner, bilingual to his monolingual, leader (at first) to his follower. Thus the attraction was to what he had despite his vulnerabilities, what he had and I have always wanted. My attraction was to something I can sometimes taste but never own, not completely and securely. It was to a certain kind of freedom. The freedom to walk alone, to be alone but not lonely, to think alone while looking out toward the horizon, and watching the waves, and feeling the grains of sand shift under my bare feet.

While my moment walking alone on the beach felt stolen, a snatched opportunity, his was a birthright.

Twilight

(*California, 2007*)

I t was the twilight hour that I identified during my years of
clubbing and drinking and smoking, of dancing and flirting,
as synonymous with a magical hour, one rife with possibility
and potential, enchanted. I've always been moved by the Golden
Gate Bridge at dusk, the rusty red of its Art Deco pillars
deepening in the waning light of the day, the blending horizon
of bay and sky serving as a vivid backdrop in shifting tones of
blue — azure, sapphire, violet. As a teenager, driving across the
bridge on weekends with friends, the cityscape glowed before
us in the setting sun, promising adventure and romance.

One night I lay in bed next to my younger son, to whom I
had been reading so he could fall asleep. As he began to drift
off, I picked up my own book, *Twilight*. On the narrow lower
bunk with my sleeping child, the lamp giving off its soft light, I
read on without pause, turning page after page. Obsessed, I
ignored my rational mind when it urged me to join my husband
in our room to sleep, reminding me that I had to wake early for
the school day rush.

When the movie came out a few months later, I fell in love
with Edward Cullen, the vampire hero of the story. *What's this
about?* I wondered then. *Perhaps a weird infatuation, a kind of
midlife crisis?* Instead of buying an expensive sports car like the
stereotypical man, I reasoned to myself, or having a flirtation or

romance, I was having an affair—an intense, long-distance, emotional affair. But this affair was not with a pen pal or a tourist from another country met on a tropical vacation, nor was it with a high school boyfriend found through the internet. Instead, despite its intensity, it was many times removed—an affair with a character in a book as embodied on the screen.

Recently, years after my "affair" with Edward Cullen, I found myself thinking again about my crush on that screen icon. I had a new perspective this time. I realized *Twilight* had it all: Edward, the mysterious, inaccessible, handsome prince. Bella, the shy, awkward, yet ultimately worthy heroine. The rescue of the maiden by the hero. Love at first sight. And what I did not see in my husband—what Edward, openly and passionately as well as constantly, demonstrated to Bella: unconditional love. Was my private, fantastical midlife crisis a midmarriage crisis? After all, I'd been with my husband for twenty-three years by then, married for sixteen. Like a teenager again, was I yearning for what Edward gave to Bella with every look, word, and touch?

Bella's mother: *There's something . . . strange about the way you two are together. The way he watches you—it's so protective. Like he's about to throw himself in front of a bullet to save you or something.*

That was the difference, I thought to myself, the fundamental difference that had had me yearning for this fictional hero. What Edward Cullen always gave Bella Swann was unshakeable devotion. What I felt from my husband at that time, whether accurate or not, was more like blithe complacency. While Bella had the prince of the high school irresistibly drawn to her despite her awkwardness, I had a husband who sighed his complaint when I cooked chicken thighs for dinner instead of breasts. While Bella had a hero use his superhuman strength to stop a Jeep from crushing her, I had a husband who didn't check in for hours when I lay in the bedroom with the flu, miserable and (I was positive) dehydrated.

Even as I analyzed my strange crush, I knew I was living a well-worn trope. Of course, in real life, any relationship has its ups and downs, its ebbs and flows, and no romantic bond can sustain the high of that initial rush when any interaction is all about the magnetic pull of the—as yet—mysterious and unknown.

Around this time, I was witnessing what I've come to see as a possible stage in life that can follow college, marriage, and babies: divorce. Almost two-thirds of the families in my son's elementary school class broke apart because of boredom, infidelity, or financial stress. People moved and emailed their new addresses; some tried online dating and spent their free evenings having sex with strangers. Among my friends there was talk of dissatisfaction and disappointment, with fantasies of separation, if not divorce.

One friend explained how she wished her husband would move into another house altogether—within driving distance, but outside the home they shared with their three young sons. "He's so grumpy all the time," she said. "It's horrible to live with. He brings us all down." A school mother told me she'd moved from the home she lived in with her husband and teenagers to a new house in the same neighborhood she'd bought for herself. "The other day I was sitting in my kitchen and I was so happy looking at the bowl of fruit on the table. Don doesn't like fruit, so we never had any around, even though I love it." She wanted to make sure, however, that I understood she wasn't divorced, that she still loved her husband. She just didn't want to live with him. Then there was my cousin who daydreamed about having her husband live in an apartment near his office during the week. "That way," she said, "he can come home on the weekends and he won't be in a bad mood about work. He can pay attention to the children. Right now—between work and the pub—all we get when he's home is an empty husk."

Edward to Bella: *You are my life*.

The lovely in-between time of the twilight hour, not quite day with its prosaic realities, not quite night with its shadows hiding sins and suffering, attracted me for its promise—the potential, held as within a golden egg, of the indefinite. Like the horizon, there was a luminosity for me in the glowing half-light of dusk. Yet, I realize now, no more. The door is shut. I chose one path.

The other day, decades after I first met my husband on New Year's Eve of 1984, a friend and I were talking, as we often do, about the past, and the paths our lives have taken, and our choices. We wondered if, going back in time, we would marry our husbands again. I thought about the children, the world unimaginable without them; the easy bonds between my husband and my family, difficult to conceive of with a person less international and traveled; the overlaps in intellectual ambition, political values, life goals.

Yes, I think to myself. Of course I would. Despite the many unknowns, the host of variables. Still, there remains, at times, a wanting. So now, I'm determined to try something different. I've lived and listed the hard parts, the annoyances as well as hurts. There are people I know who seem to special-ize in resentment-gathering. Like squirrels with nuts, they pounce on any perceived slight or insult; they collect them with care, hoarding them in an ever-increasing pile somewhere deep inside where they will not only be safe but also grow and multiply. I don't want to be that kind of squirrely person, con-stantly on the lookout for what to interpret as an injury and take offense from.

I read a happiness-generating technique. Its instructions are to write, pen to paper or keyboard to screen, the positive in any given situation. A career. A relocation. A marriage. Anything, however small. Hate your job and can't think of anything to like about it? Well, do you get paid? There it is: have gratitude for making money. Be grateful for that, even if for the time being, even if for the moment. Does the tree in your back garden shed too much every winter so that you grumble about having to rake all those fallen leaves? Think instead about the cool shade this tree provides every summer with those very same leaves, the shade that is always better, deeper, more profound somehow, than the shade from the side of the house or a patio umbrella.

I like this exercise; it's not a new idea, really, but a useful reminder to live a happier life. I share it with my friend. We decide to deliberately seek, as if smooth stones and intact shells on a beach, the good that exists in life. For me, it's the gift of a hand-woven rug carried from Northern Pakistan to Afghanistan to San Francisco, the gentle eyelid kisses during a hospital stay, the box of glowing tulips from Seattle opened in Marin County. The laughter into the darkness from our bed at a funny comment or a ridiculous dream in the middle of the night. Mimicking to one another the mispronunciations of English idioms by my Spanish-speaking grandmother or his Arabic-speaking father. The tradition of eating dinner, plates balanced on laps, while watching a Masterpiece Theater drama. Listening together through a door ajar to a son playing a Chopin nocturne. Marveling at the hummingbirds who collect every summer, a dazzling pink and green, to sip the nectar from the purple sage we've planted especially to attract them. Overhearing my husband telling our children that their mother's favorite time of day is twilight.

Seatmates

(*US, 2019*)

I squeeze by the two people occupying seats 27C and 27B as they contort their bodies, angling their knees to one side to give me enough space with a minimum of upheaval. Despite their efforts, I have to sidle past their legs—head bent to avoid hitting the low ceiling, one arm ready to grab a seat back for balance, the other clutching the tote that holds a folded pashmina, my makeup bag, a water bottle, and two books.

Finally, I flop into my seat, 27A; simply reaching this cramped space I'll occupy for the next five hours has felt like an acrobatic feat.

Still, I feel lucky—booked on Southwest, my husband and I had neglected to go online twenty-four hours ahead to reserve space in the coveted A group, the one that boards before groups B and C, and thus were two of the last people to enter the plane. My husband, however, spied an empty window seat he knows to be my favorite kind and quickly pointed it out for me while he went on to the back with my roll-on, most probably to claim an unwanted middle seat after wrangling for space above.

I settle in next to the couple beside me, buckling my seatbelt, unfolding my black scarf and wrapping its softness around me, taking a motion sickness pill with a sip from my bottle of water, placing a novel on my lap. When I proceed to spray moist towelettes with lavender and wipe down my seat, a habit since the days of battling head lice when my children were in elementary school, the young woman next to me exclaims, "That's *such* a good idea—I should remember to do that!"

I'm quick to offer her some wipes, which she accepts gratefully, and I spray them liberally with scent before handing them over.

Sitting by the couple, I can feel their good mood, their lightness of being. There's an undercurrent of excitement and joie de vivre in their body language. Apropos of nothing, the woman turns and embraces the man. He hugs her back. They both, I notice with my peripheral vision, try to make as much contact as possible—arm to arm, cheek to cheek, forehead to forehead. They sit thus for a while before their high spirits separate them and they begin to chat animatedly.

The young woman, maybe thirty, her blonde hair bouncing with health, wears white and pink spandex—a fitted jacket with tight leggings—and trendy sneakers. She turns to her partner, a slender, bearded man in jeans and a pale sweatshirt, and notes, "Hey, this is the first time I've been on a plane without Teddy." I assume he asks her how she feels about this; I cannot know for sure since he's further away and his voice is muffled. She seems ambivalent, but happier than sad. She says she feels "freer, I guess."

I wonder if Teddy is their child. I strain my limited vision, trying to angle my head so I can see their left hands without being obvious. No, no wedding rings. Teddy must be her son then. My assumption is confirmed when I see, again through sidelong glances, that her phone's screensaver exhibits a picture of a small blond boy, posed alone, beaming at the camera.

As they talk between looking at their phones, adjusting their seatbelts, and shifting positions, they often hold hands, lean into each other, caress one another. I imagine they are a fairly solid couple, close but not engaged, involved but not living together. I am cynical—they wouldn't display such affection if not for the still-present thrill of romance, the titillation of mystery. They have yet, I'm sure, to discover the annoying habits of the other, the irritations of different routines—from bedtime rituals to bathroom hygiene. Does she know he leaves the toilet seat up, the toothpaste cap off, his dirty clothes on the floor? Does he know she tends to nag about dishwashing and laundry folding? That she holds sacred her son's diet restrictions and screen-time limits? Do they know one of them is a night owl and the other an early riser? They seem to me so enmeshed, like a tightly woven tapestry—one that tells the tale of new love, true love, romantic love. They seem carefree, unweighted by daily concerns or mundane worries that morph into friction, into the stress that wears on the weave of love and romance, threatening to unravel the promise of happily-ever-after.

Listening to them through the drone of the engines, glancing at them occasionally through a fog of drowsiness, I feel a nostalgia tinged with more than the usual sadness. Was I there once, with my husband? I know we're not there now. I know also what the experts say and the experienced couples corroborate—that romance is fleeting, that the real "work" of a relationship, moving past the surface frustrations and petty annoyances to know and value and love the real person, what lies underneath, their essence and their core, comes later. Have we succeeded in accomplishing this? We, my husband and I, remind me of the country duet about islands in a stream, but instead of islands we are the stream, trying to negotiate the fallen tree trunks and sunken rowboats, the craggy boulders and sharp rocks that lie in wait to snag our mutually crafted tapestry of togetherness, that separate us as we strive to preserve the flow of our lives and our love around such obstacles and come together again.

Soon after the flight attendant announces the need to fasten seatbelts and prepare for arrival, there's a notable shift in the interaction between my seatmates. He shows her a text on his phone. Since I can't see his face or hear his voice, I'm not prepared for the negative reaction it elicits. She sits up, stiff, and draws away from him. Taking the phone in her own hand to peer more closely at the words on the screen, she whispers a series of questions with a frown, her tone icy and her demeanor accusatory. He defends himself, still soft-spoken. She attacks and he responds. She is the one who seems to hold the moral ground; I don't know if this is justified. All I know is that I have been there. I've been driven to bait and strike, to bicker and quarrel—driven by anger, frustration, indignation, or pain. I've felt slighted, put upon, maltreated, hurt.

Yet watching this couple, these two younger people who've been my neighbors for the five-hour flight, I want to say, *Stop! Don't ruin the moment. Don't squander happiness.* Even though I know how seriously I've taken my own resentments in the past, I still want to say, *It's not worth it in the end. Don't let petty grievances separate you.* I know it's always easier on the outside looking in; I know how hard it is on the inside, in the middle, unable to see a way out. The young woman whom I am judging may very well be regretting her words as she says them, she may be telling herself to calm down, not to make such a big deal of this text and the offense implied therein. But she is simultaneously caught in the trap of vexation and accumulated animosity. I know I have been.

I traveled once, when newly married, to a land foreign to me with my husband and his parents. There were sand dunes and golden ruins begging to be photographed. I'd packed my camera, eagerly anticipating such a moment. But my new husband grabbed it before I could, and darted off among the dunes and ruins, clicking away from what he considered the most advantageous angles.

I was furious. How dared he? It was *my* camera; *I* packed it, *I* wanted to be in control of the photos.

With silence and scowls, I made my displeasure known. My husband blithely ignored me until he'd snapped enough pictures to satisfy himself. But by then I could no longer be placated with command of the camera or even open apologies. My mood remained dark and angry, I silent and sulky.

Later, in the chauffeured car, my mother-in-law tried to make peace between her son and his wife, taking our hands and placing them together. "You must always love each other," she said. I removed my hand, thinking only of my husband's selfishness.

As the engines roar and whine while switching gears from cruise to descent, I imagine the couple surviving this spat, and others like it, to marry. I feel I know what the wedding would look like: probably in a picturesque barn, young hipster groomsmen in matching beards and undersized suits with carefully curated lagers in hand. The women are similarly young, their lace and chiffon gowns bohemian chic. Some may already be married, and attend with their infants in tow. There might be two cakes, a plain chocolate one for the groom, a frothier vanilla one for the bride. Thinking about these two, rigid with tension by my side, I predict cake-smearing to the squeals and laughter of their audience—no careful feeding of each other, which signifies (according to the superstitious) respectful relations to come. But I can't see past the ceremony. Will they survive as a couple? A unit? A team? Will he be able to include her son in his definition of family? Will her issues with relationships (I wonder where is the father of her son) cause this new bond to fray over time? Will there be a half-sister or brother for Teddy?

As the plane slowly descends, the future couple in my imagination fades and the real couple next to me lapses into silence. She is angry. She refuses to turn toward her partner, to engage in chitchat, to smile. Once I see his hand approach her tentatively before coming to a rest, lightly, questioningly, on her spandexed thigh. He leaves it there for a moment, hopeful. But she pretends not to notice and he retreats, pulling his hand back, chastened.

After landing with a bump and a screech, the plane slows to a stop and I lose sight of my seatmates in the flurry of announcements by cheerful flight attendants, the snap of safety belts removed, the click of overhead bins opened. I wait for the activity to die down and the jammed aisle to empty before I make my way to the front of the aircraft, loath to join the herd.

Outside the plane, my husband waits for me patiently, my disembarking routine familiar to him. The roll-on he has retrieved for me sits at his feet. I greet him with a smile and, wordlessly, we walk together through the jet bridge on our way out. I have my last sighting of my former seatmates near the baggage claim area. Facing away from each other, she sits while he stands, both on their phones, their expressions stony. My husband and I walk by the couple as if they were two islands in our stream, separating only momentarily before coming together again as we continue to our car and leave them behind.

Children

(*California, 2021*)

"We should have them," my husband said.

It was a dark and stormy night (I know, I know, but it really was) in the winter of 1997 as we hurtled down the interstate from Boston to New York in the cocoon that a car can become of leather seats, dim dashboard light, and radio music. The wipers were on, doing double duty in the dense rain that lashed at us with the wind and our speed.

"If we don't, we'll regret it," he added.

We were discussing children. Whether to have them or not. I was still inclined toward no. My husband was leaning, more and more heavily, on yes. It was a serious discussion, the most serious we'd ever had on the subject.

These days I always see myself in this scene from the past as driving, and maybe I was, since both my husband and I love to drive. But it could also have been him—it was, after all, dark with night and rain, and I may have chosen the passenger seat as easier, cozier. Yet my memory insists on the driver's seat, my hands on the wheel, in control, with agency, with the ultimate agency—over life and death—that driving a bulk of metal at seventy-five miles per hour in a storm can give you.

"But," I said, "it's such a horrible world."

"We can bring up our children to be good citizens to make it better," he parried.

"I don't want to sacrifice my children to a cause," I answered, suddenly passionate in defense of my unconceived, unborn offspring, "and probably an impossible cause."

Years before, younger, and immature, I'd declared to my friends my intention of having either no children or six. Nothing in between. The drama of extremes pleased me. I didn't want to be ordinary. One friend wanted six boys (I don't know why the number six was so popular among us), no girls. That was her claim to drama, to the extraordinary. Before that, even younger, I had thought three the ideal number of children because I had two siblings and I favored what I knew, what felt familiar and safe.

I asked my husband if he thought more people in the world were happy than sad. Looking back, this question sounds like a riddle in a fable or a fairy tale. Yet he remained undeterred.

"Yes," he answered. "For sure more than fifty percent of people are happier in general than sad."

My own store of knowledge ran through my head at this point: *The Dalai Lama says we see only the bad news on television. We don't see the million acts of kindness occurring all over the world, every day. These are much less newsworthy.*

"But what about the environment?" I asked out loud, a final objection. Those were the early days still, at least for the general public, of climate change worry; we knew it simply as "global warming."

In response, my husband brought up what passed then for a solution—one solution at least to our conundrum, a rationalization for having children in an overpopulated planet: "We'll just have two," he said, "one to replace me, another to replace you. We won't be adding to the population that way."

N early two decades later, I have two grown sons. It's late August, and although my youngest already moved to his college thirty minutes away, he's come back for the afternoon to partake in the family ritual of watching preseason football at his grandparents' house down the road. Rather than accompany my husband in driving my son back to his dorm, I decide to stay home. Sitting on the stone bench by the side of the house, near the garage doors, I wave as they back out of the driveway, blowing my son a kiss.

The past few days my husband and I have been bickering constantly in front of this youngest son—not raising our voices but vying for dominance, for control, for the last word. We are stressed, our psyches challenged, our nerves stretched by the process of moving him into his dorm room. His university is just a bridge and a bay away, yet this milestone, with its symbolic significance, weighs on us. A certain stage for our family, when the four of us were all under one roof, when I would wake in the morning and listen for voices and footsteps, when I would offer my sons breakfasts of eggs or French toast and force them to drink the sludgy green smoothies I carefully blended every day, is done. This stage is over in any consistent way, teatimes on the sunny patio in the summer or by the gas fire in the winter relegated to vacations and stolen, in-between days.

People say a child leaving home is hardest on the mother, but in our case it is an equal-opportunity moment for suffering. Hence the sadness that manifests in irritation and argument. Yet I envy my husband. I believe he's in a better position than me to handle our new reality of empty nest. He has a job— more than a job, a career. He's busy many hours of most days. He contributes to society with his energy and his effort; he is valued for this contribution. Could I have tried harder to get a teaching job after I had children, after we moved back to California from Seattle to be closer to our parents? Part of my choice of career, when I was in college and before we were married, was the time it would give me during school breaks to be with the children I might have in the future. Yet I suspect that even if I were to go back in time, I would do the same, for it seems I have a compulsion to nurture my children, to be with them as much as possible, especially if any time away from them would be spent at a low-paying adjunct position. So I elected to stay home while my husband worked for our living, and, this afternoon, I elect to stay home while my husband drives our younger son back to his dorm. It will be better this way, I reason. He won't have us arguing as he sits in the back of the car about what area rug he should get for his room or when to research extracurriculars like wrestling and 49ers fandom. We both think we know best; we both are desperate to influence him according to that knowledge. Plus, I have to wash my hair.

Some days ago I emailed friends from a book group. We hadn't met for over a year due to shutdowns and social distancing. Could we get together? For coffee or dinner to catch up? I told them my dread of the silent empty nest.

Before I could begin to regret the neediness in my tone, all of them answered. *Yes!* they said. One spoke of facing a similar situation. Another tried to comfort with talk of yet-undefined silver linings (I'm skeptical, sure she has a cat rather than children). I'm glad I emailed, happy I will soon have those few hours of distraction and camaraderie; I feel an urgent need to fill the days and weeks ahead.

Because we are alone again, my husband and I. For what seems like the first time, but is, in reality, again. That's how we started, after all. Alone, as a couple. First in a suburban house too large for us that his parents bought for him when he moved north for residency; then, after I joined him, in an apartment with a city view that suited me better; then, for our fellowship year, one in an eastern city with a garden view in an old converted manor house, an actual suit of armor on silent duty in the wood-paneled lobby. We came together, married, lived with each other for seven years, and then multiplied (or, rather, doubled).

After hearing about "Empty Nest Parties" that some parents in the US hold to celebrate their last child leaving the house, leaving them to their space and their uninterrupted routines and their private rituals of romance or cleaning or TV watching, I begin to collect stories of communal living. Of extended family compounds. Of children returning to the family home or neighborhood or city after college, sometimes with higher degrees and spouses and jobs.

This last summer, the summer after my youngest son's graduation from high school, we took a trip as a family to visit friends in South Carolina. There we toured Gullah country, an island owned by the descendants of enslaved people, with a culture preserved over the centuries by the inaccessibility of the island until a bridge was built, relatively recently, connecting it to the mainland. From the air-conditioned van I stared out the window as our grandmotherly tour guide explained that the groups of houses we saw on the various properties lining the road were called "clusters." I immediately felt a sympathetic pull, and also—a pang of envy. A cluster is the name the Gullah have for a complex with family homes built close to one another, mere yards away from each other, on flat common property, sometimes an acre, sometimes two. Here live different nuclear families within the larger extended family group—grandparents and children and grandchildren, aunts and uncles and cousins. Each family has its own house, its own kitchen and bedrooms and bathrooms, but shares yard space, vegetable gardens, lawn, and sitting areas.

I'm walking with a friend near her neighborhood in our county when she points out a property she knows.

"Look at that," she says, gesturing toward two long single-story buildings facing each other over a wide gravel strip. "It has about four units."

I look, absorbing the information, and immediately start making the space over to my specifications, imagining what I would do if it were mine. I see myself, my children, and their future families living in the units. I see cypresses growing in rows flanking a wrought iron gate, bounding the space and making it cozy with their dense green. I see a fountain at the opposite end of the gate and a flagstone path winding its way from little round tables and wrought iron chairs to garden nooks with ferns in the shade and lavender in the sun. I see two and then three generations living in that one shared space, with opportunities for community and privacy, for both socializing and quiet.

In the past few years I've had many conversations with different friends regarding our lack of knowledge about certain aspects of parenthood. We discuss never having been warned. I did know, however, first from almost a decade of babysitting and later from religiously reading books like *What to Expect When You're Expecting*, what pregnancy and labor and delivery might feel like. I thought I had a good grasp on how hard it might be to look after a tiny baby twenty-four hours a day, seven days a week—to be responsible for its safety, health, sustenance, and growth. The stages after toddlerhood were more hazy in my imagination, yet I was confident they would be filled with orderly years of teachers and schools, piano lessons and home-work.

What no one warned us about, my friends and I agree, was the sacrifice required in letting go: in encouraging a child to apply to colleges (even those far away) and subsequently leave home, in watching that child pack his clothes and board a plane to live apart from his parents for months at a time, maybe forever. When deciding whether or not to have children in the first place, it wasn't sacrifice that I thought about, it was selfishness. Over and over I asked myself, was it selfish to insist on bringing more children into this world? The stress involved in bringing up a child, in trying to raise him to be his best and his happiest, never factored into my plans.

I slide over the stretch of fitted sheet that separates me from my husband. It's the first night we are alone after a summer of boy energy, loads of sweaty laundry, the taking-over of the garage by kettlebells and weights, the smells of chicken or garlic permeating the house from experimental forays into cooking.

I slide over carefully, as quietly as possible, so as not to wake him. I've stayed up later than him, reading by lamplight, and it's a cold night—or so he announced when he first came to bed, complaining about the cooled night air typical of the summers in Northern California. He regretted the absence of his precious wintertime heating pad as he snuggled down under the duvet we share. I, on the other hand, run hot these days. Hot flashes keep me from any kind of consistent comfort, and this night, as usual, I've lain in bed in camisole pajamas, bare arms over the blanket, holding my copy of *Wives and Daughters*. This novel, nostalgic itself for the generation before its own time, comforts with its familiar, domestic tale of widowers and their devoted daughters, remarriage and stepparents, filial duty and family loyalty in a small English village almost exactly two hundred years ago. It feeds my aesthetic sensibilities with descriptions of candlelit dinners and flaming logs crackling in cavernous stone fireplaces, or of climbing roses outside open parlor windows and afternoon tea on white linen tablecloths. It's a balm on sore skin to enter this world far away from my own worries, where I know what happens—where I can be sure of a happy ending.

I used to run cold. Before all the hot flashing. So I'm familiar with that shivery sensation, with pricking fingers of ice up and down arms, legs, even ears. Gingerly, before the next hot flash, I approach my sleeping husband, who is curled on his side to capture the warmth within his folded limbs. I slide my legs up against his, bending them so our bodies approximate an apostrophe, knowing that my thighs are warm enough because they've been under the covers as I read. Then I slip my bare and, I'm well aware, icy arm over his chest, trying not to touch any of his warm skin but to stay instead on the material of his T-shirt, and hug him gently to me.

He moves, so I try to retract my arm, but in a second he grabs my hand and pulls me closer to him.

F is for . . .

(*Los Angeles, 2018*)

I was at a funeral that was more like a memorial, for the cremation had occurred weeks before, and instead of a body to bury there were photographs and flowers and speeches. So F in this case is not for Funeral, or even Funereal for that matter. Because I would also venture to claim that this memorial was not typical, although I haven't been to many memorials and therefore am not an expert. There was an air of socializing and celebration that included drinking, music, and dancing. The guests were mostly young, or liked to think of themselves as young. Among them were men in baseball caps holding beer cans, women in jeans and flowered tops. A few were dressed more soberly, as I was, in darker colors, longer skirts, and high heels rather than sandals or wedges. Although some guests were actually in their twenties and thirties, most were middle-aged like me but had come ready to celebrate my friend's father and his well-lived life rather than mourn his death.

Renee, my friend, had arranged this memorial: she had selected a date, invited the guests, ordered the clusters of beribboned white roses placed around the house and the backyard, set up the mic for speeches and toasts. It felt like a blend of wedding, funeral reception, and Fourth of July party.

She lives in Southern California, so the day was warm and the sun shone unimpeded on the garden and the pool.

I found myself a chair at a table outside, where I spent some time chatting with an elderly guest and her two adult children, a son and a daughter. She had shortish white hair and all the sags and wrinkles that time, genes, and gravity can give. This woman had, quite intrepidly for her generation, left England alone in her youth, when barely an adult, and emigrated to the United States to make her fortune here. It was then that she'd met my friend's father, and subsequently shared a history of friendship with him and his wife for decades afterward.

As I listened to her story, another guest approached our table and asked, before drawing back a chair, if it was "okay" for her to sit with us.

"Yes, of course—join us!" we replied, eager to make this girl comfortable. For she looked like a girl; she was young, maybe twenty. She gave the impression of a colt, skinny rather than thin, gangly-limbed and long-necked. Her black jacket, a single-breasted blazer hanging loosely from her narrow shoulders, looked too big for her small frame. Her hair, long and yellow, lay flat against her head. She had big eyes that seemed always open wide on high alert, almost skittish. She sat with us, not speaking, simply watching and listening. She stared mostly at me as I talked; her large eyes, a light swimming pool blue, almost obsessively tracked my gestures and expressions.

Then the conversation turned. I don't remember now what came before it, only that it was I who steered it in a new direction by announcing to the table that I was a "raging feminist." This was not the first time I'd declared my politicized identity thus. The world I grew up in—my family, for example, as well as the academia where I wrote, published, and taught—existed in another era. In that world, in those days, there was pressure to be careful of what I said, to study my audience before I spoke; my reality was a battlefield where I, as a feminist, defended the intersection of my identity as a woman and a Latina. It had therefore become habitual for me to declare my stance, feet planted, sword drawn, ready to protect my very Self. In this case, I had a mixed audience—if not at this table, where a fourth guest had just seated himself, then definitely at the memorial in general. I was also in the habit of considering my feminism a weak and fragile creature, a creature that had been battered from all sides its whole existence, and therefore something I, as its creator, its hostess, its constantly vigilant protector, had to nurture and strengthen and support through open, steadfast allegiance.

In the middle of my next sentence, the slim, delicate girl interrupted me. This was the first time she'd spoken since telling us her name and that she knew Renee, the daughter of the deceased, from work. "You're a *feminist*?" she asked, sliding forward in her seat, her face eager. It was as if she had suddenly come alive, my pronouncement a spark that flared and then surged through her body, animating the hidden passion within her.

What did I say in response? A simple *yes*? Perhaps a *Yes, absolutely*, or a reiterative *Yes, and don't forget, a raging one*. But I replied in the affirmative, that I'm sure of, for this shy girl— quiet, thin, and fragile-looking—lifted her arms from her sides in response, fists clenched in a gesture of strength, skinny wrists finally exposed from under her jacket's too-long sleeves, and joyfully, jubilantly, proclaimed, "I am too!"

It's hard to describe the effect this young woman's sudden exclamation, her delighted statement, had on me. The triumph, the exultation, the almost gleeful surprise in her gestures and tone—they were at once gratifying, comprising a victorious moment for me, a woman twice her age, a somewhat cynical veteran of the sex wars, of gendered resistance, and appalling. For how could a young person, clearly thoughtful about her identity as a woman, as a female in this world, still live in a reality where a fellow feminist, proud and outspoken, could come as a surprise, an anomaly, a sort of treasure unexpectedly uncovered?

I responded by affirming in strong terms her desire for a teammate, a sister in solidarity, an ally. *Yes* and *Of course* and *Shouldn't everyone be?*

It felt good as well to get such an unequivocally positive reaction to my proclaimed identity. I'd experienced in the past the sudden awkward silences, the confused grimaces, even the angry frowns in reaction to my declaring myself a feminist, regardless of whether it was more an acknowledgment than a declaration, or made in a voice quiet and insecure rather than defiant and challenging. My relatives in Peru looked at me as if I were an alien, a monster suddenly sitting in their midst, a Medusa who'd abruptly sprouted snakes from her head whenever I brought up animal rights, civil rights, women's rights—any kind of rights. I eventually stopped trying to talk with them about rights altogether. In a graduate class a male student spoke of the women in Shakespeare's plays as "chicks." It never occurred to me then to speak aloud my discomfort with his language. But a female student didn't have a problem calling it out. *"What?"* she asked, sarcastic and contemptuous. "Women as *poultry?*" With my husband's colleagues I became accustomed to approaching the subject of gendered inequality obliquely, perhaps talking about my educational goals, or my belief not just in longer maternity leave but also paternity leave, or my admiration for the country of Finland, which had for many years a lesbian president. I grew up hearing my father telling me *don't be strident* when I defended my position against his, or my mother laughingly calling me *un sargento* when I angrily made a point in a family argument. Those words—*strident* and *sergeant*—have encoded in them the idea that speaking one's mind, defending one's position, is inherently unfeminine.

Maybe that's why I learned to love the word *feminist*, even though I quickly became used to hearing it spoken as if a dirty word—a shameful one, ugly and grotesque. For to me *feminist* defies expectations; it declares that to be firm in one's convictions, trying always to speak one's truth, is inherently feminine. It belongs to the reality, the identity, the selfhood, of woman. Woman as whole, productive, creative, legitimate. Woman as person. Woman as human.

I read in that young guest's face a relief I'd experienced before. To assume one has to tiptoe around, careful not to make too much sound, not to disturb, as if walking on eggshells that might at any moment, with any false move, crack and break beneath clumsy feet, and then to discover that such care, such self-circumscription and self-censorship, isn't necessary because there's someone close by who thinks as one does, who believes as one does, is like being pulled into a lifeboat by a gentle coastguard from a stormy sea where one has felt abandoned and alone.

So what is the moral of this story? I know what it is for me. That F is for Feminism. It is my defining discourse, my moral compass. I don't care if my passion seems melodramatic or hysterical (I'm well aware there still exist in our world these tired, dangerous tropes). The animating spark in my life may have been watching the interactions between my parents, absorbing the emotions of conflict I felt palpably around me. This spark, going forward, fed on both nature and nurture, genes and experience. F, then, is also for Forward into the Future. For Fighting the good Fight. F to me is for Favorite— feminism as my favorite philosophy, my favorite ideology, my favorite identity.

Because F is also for Fantastic and Fabulous and Fierce and Freeing. Feminism as formative ideology and discourse of freedom has been a site of strength as well as struggle, it has

been the place from which I've been able to envision a positive way of being, an empowered Self. I could have said, to
the young woman sitting at the table, *I'm a fierce feminist*, with
similar results. Watching this shy young person, one who'd
heretofore barely spoken, lift her arms in triumph, and then in
a flash understanding that she felt isolated in her evolving
feminism, that she was relieved to discover that others around
her could be feminists too, proudly and unapologetically so,
made all that had come before—the struggle and outrage, the
embarrassment and awkwardness—worth it. The years of
keeping quiet in conservative circles; of the pressure to be
more feminist, to act more like a feminist; of attempting to
speak out, sometimes after much inner struggle; of learning to
live my values and principles, to express myself with my own
voice—all of it, ultimately, worth it.

F is for Feminism, and always will be.

To Be Continued . . .

Source Acknowledgments

Parts of this book were previously published, sometimes in slightly different form or with different titles, in the following publications: "Breasts" in *Narrative Magazine*, "The Flawed Fairy Tale" in *The Acentos Review*, "The Sandal" and "Ten Dollars" in *The Nasiona*, "There Is a Way Out" in *HerStry*, "Wrinkles" in *The Woven Tale Press*, "Kept Woman" in *Pangyrus*, and "León" in *Dorothy Parker's Ashes*.

This book includes quotes or references from Gloria Anzaldúa, *Borderlands/La Frontera: The New Mestiza*, Aunt Lute Books, 2006.

Acknowledgments

I am eternally grateful to Natasha Singh, first and dear reader. Thank you to Marion Roach Smith, for setting me on the right track at the very beginning. To Suzanne Sherman for her thoughtful feedback. To Kathleen McClung, who taught me so much, and all my classmates at San Francisco's Writing Salon for their constant encouragement. To Wendy Dale, Tamara Dean, Lisa Cooper Ellison, Laura Fraser, Kathy Garlick, Beth Kephart, Allison Lane, Linda Joy Myers, Brooke Warner, and Allison K. Williams for their generosity in sharing their knowledge and expertise. To my sisters at She Writes Press for their ready friendship, writerly advice, and moral support. To Sonia Daccarett, my *comadre* in our (very) Tiny Writers Group, for her unwavering championship of my writing.

About the Author

Marianna Marlowe is a Latina writer of creative nonfiction that explores issues of gender identity, feminism, cultural hybridity, intersectionality, and more. Her short memoir has been published in *Narrative Magazine, Hippocampus Magazine, The Woven Tale Press, Eclectica Magazine, Sukoon Magazine,* and *The Acentos Review* among others. She lives in the San Francisco Bay Area.

Looking for your next great read?

We can help!

Visit www.shewritespress.com/next-read
or scan the QR code below for a list
of our recommended titles.

She Writes Press is an award-winning
independent publishing company founded to
serve women writers everywhere.